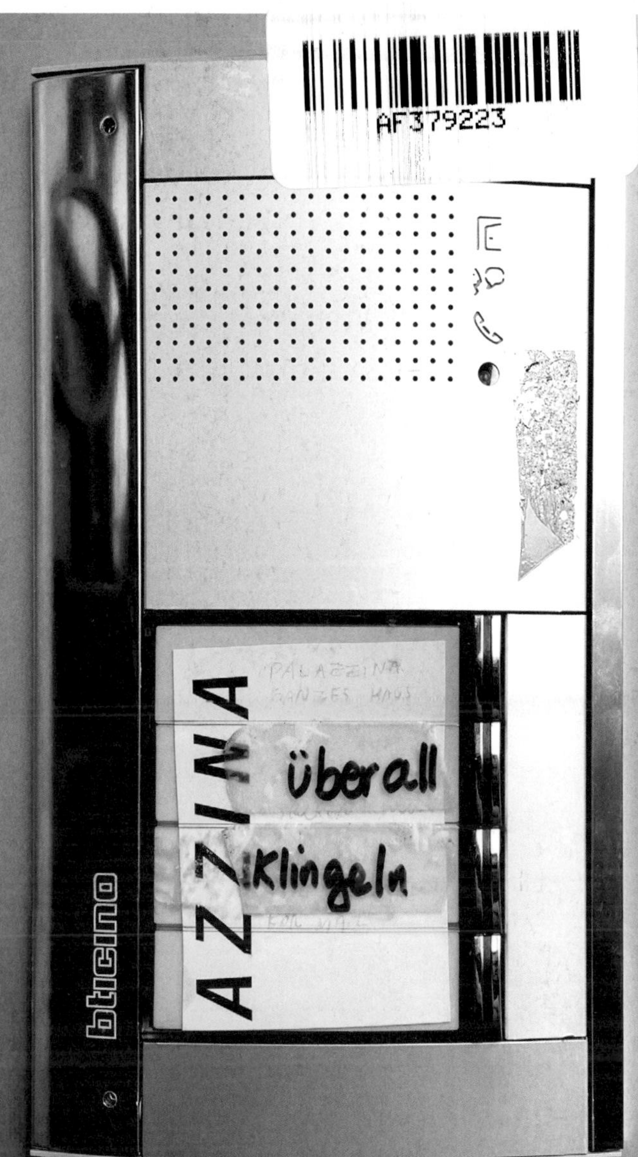
AF379223
bticino
AZZINA
PALAZZINA
GANZES HAUS
überall
Klingeln

Á. Birna Björnsdóttir ○
Adrien Chevalley
Alan Schmalz
Alex Ghandour
Amélie Bodenmann
Ana Bălan
Anastasia Pavlou
Anaïs Nariman Aïk
Andreas Dobler
Andreas Kalbermatter
Anina Müller
Anne-Laure Franchette
Baker Wardlaw
Bastien Gachet
Brigham Baker
Camilla Paolino
Camille Dumond
Camille Farrah Buhler
Camille Lacroix
Carolina Sandvik
Caroline Bachmann
Caterina De Nicola
Charles Benjamin
Chloé Delarue
Claudia & Julia Müller

Daniel Kurth
Dario Zeo
Djellza Azemi
Dominic Michel
Eli Maria Lundgaard
Elise Corpataux
Emanuel Rossetti
Ernestyna Orlowska
Ester Alemayehu
  Hatle
Francesca Mangold
Géraldine Honauer
Giada Olivotto
Gilles Jacot
Gina Proenza
Giorgia Garzilli
Grégory Sugnaux
Guadalupe Ruiz
Hanna Rochereau
Hannes Zulauf
Haydée Marin
Ines Tondar
Ingo Niermann
Ivan Mitrović
Jakub Andrzejewski

Jennifer Merlyn
  Scherler
Joan Pallé
Joaquim Cantor
  Miranda
Josefin Arnell
Judith Kakon
Julie Monot
Juliette Uzor
Kaspar Ludwig
Katrin Niedermeier
Kelly Tissot
Laim Kim
LapTopRadio
Lorraine Baylac
Lara and Noa Castro
Léa Katharina Meier
Leevi Toija
Lena Laguna Diel
Leolie Greet
Leonardo Bürgi Tenorio
Linus Weber
Lithic Alliance
Livio Casanova
Luca Rossi Dossi

Lucas Herzig
Lula Broglio
Lysann König
Madeleine Noraas
Mariana Murcia
Marilou Bal
Marisabel Arias
Marta Margnetti
Mathieu Dafflon
Mathilde Rosier
Maya Hottarek
Maïté Chénière
Melanie Akeret
Mia Sanchez
Mirjam Plattner
Mitchell Anderson
Mónica Heller
Natacha Donzé
Nicolás Sarmiento
Nina Rieben
Noemi Pfister
Núria Güell
Nusser Glazova
Paula Santomé
Pauline Coquart

Paulo Wirz
Philip Ortelli
Philémon Otth
Phoenix Atala
Ray Hegelbach
Rebecca Kunz
Remy Ugarte Vallejos
Rhona Mühlebach
Roman Selim
    Khereddine
Ronja Svaneborg
Salome Jokhadze
San Keller
Sara Gassmann
Sara Magenheimer
Sara Ravelli
Simone Holliger
Simon Fahrni
Sina Oberhänsli
Sofía Durrieu
Sophie Yerly
Séverine Heizmann
Thales Pessoa
Tim Kummer
Tiphanie Kim Mall

TJ Cuthand
Tobias Dirty
Tomás Maglione
Valentina Parati
Valentin Carron
Val Minnig
Vera Mühlebach 
Vesna Bilanović
Vicente Lesser
  Gutierrez
Victor Delétraz
Victoria Holdt
Viola Leddi
X Schneeberger
Zara Idelson
& Co.

Current member ○
Former member ⊘

Palazzina

Ring Everywhere
Überall klingeln

Mousse Publishing

Palazzina is a non-profit exhibition space and artists' house founded in 2019.

The name Palazzina is an Italian word that refers to a small residential building with multiple apartments.

The team works in close collaboration with the invited artists, dissolving the boundaries between public and private spheres.

It has hosted exhibitions in three buildings around Basel, with each location also serving as a home for its members.

The project *On Foot*
adds a flexible pavilion
that can be adapted
to a variety of exhibition
formats, without the
need for a fixed location.

palazzina.ch

Palazzina wurde 2019 als
Offspace und Künst-
ler*innenhaus gegründet.

Der Name Palazzina leitet
sich vom italienischen
Wort für ein kleines
Mehrfamilienhaus ab.

Das Team arbeitet eng
mit den eingeladenen
Künstler*innen zusammen
und verwischt dabei
die Grenzen zwischen
Öffentlichem und Priva-
tem.

Palazzina hat bereits
Ausstellungen in drei
Gebäuden in Basel
organisiert, die den Mit-
gliedern auch als Wohn-
raum dien(t)en.

Das Projekt *On Foot* erweitert das Projekt um einen flexiblen Pavillon, der sich an die unterschiedlichsten Ausstellungsformate anpassen lässt, ohne an einen festen Standort gebunden zu sein.

palazzina.ch

Exhibition Views
Selection 2019–25

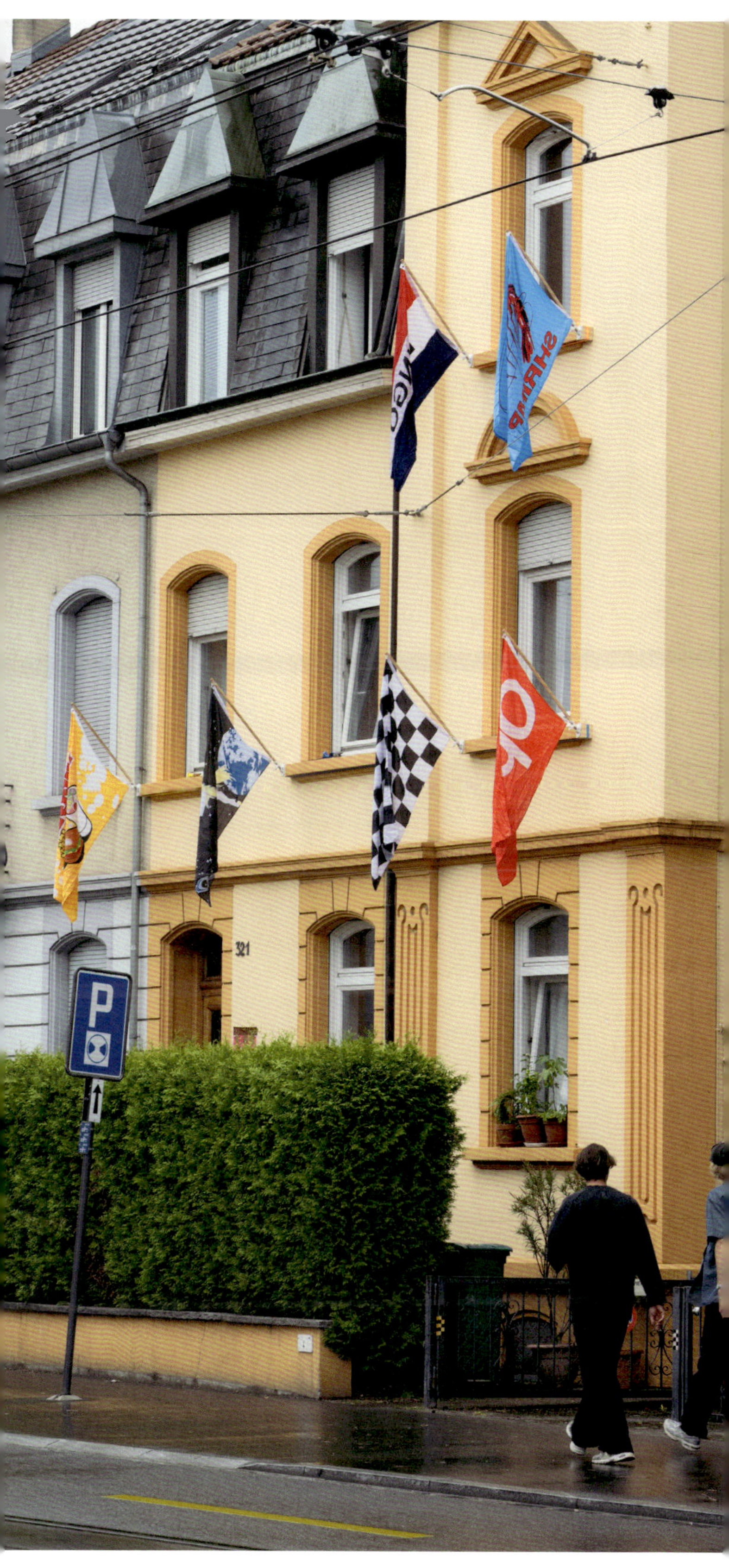

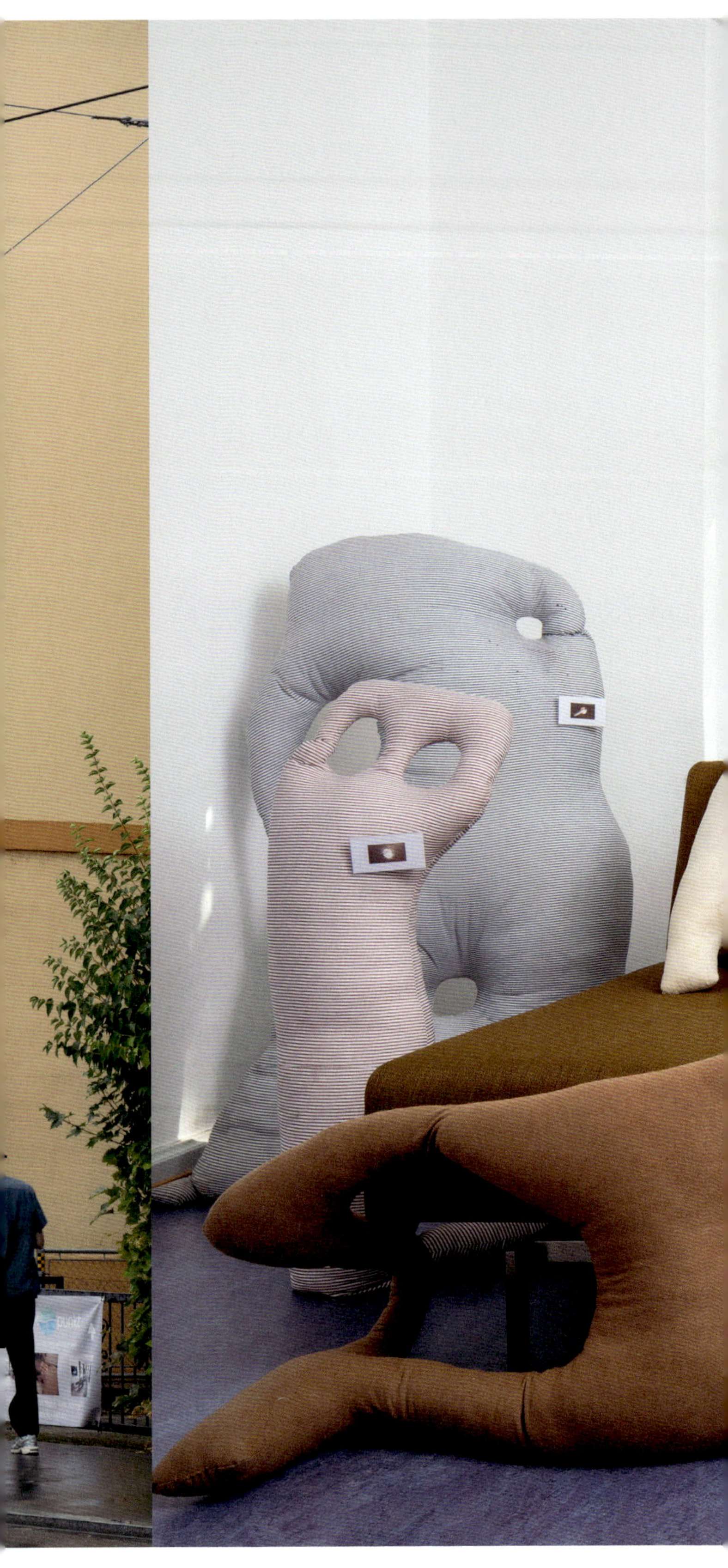

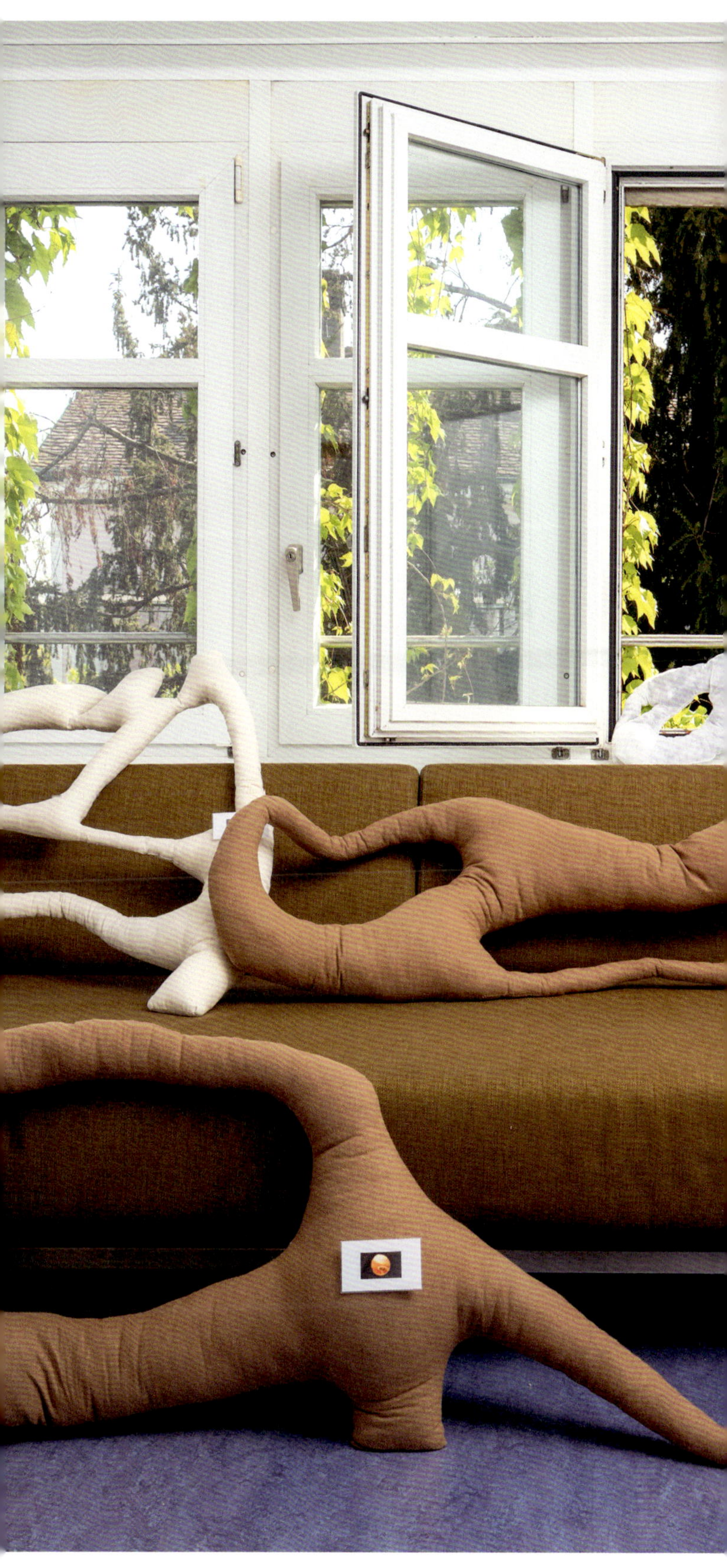

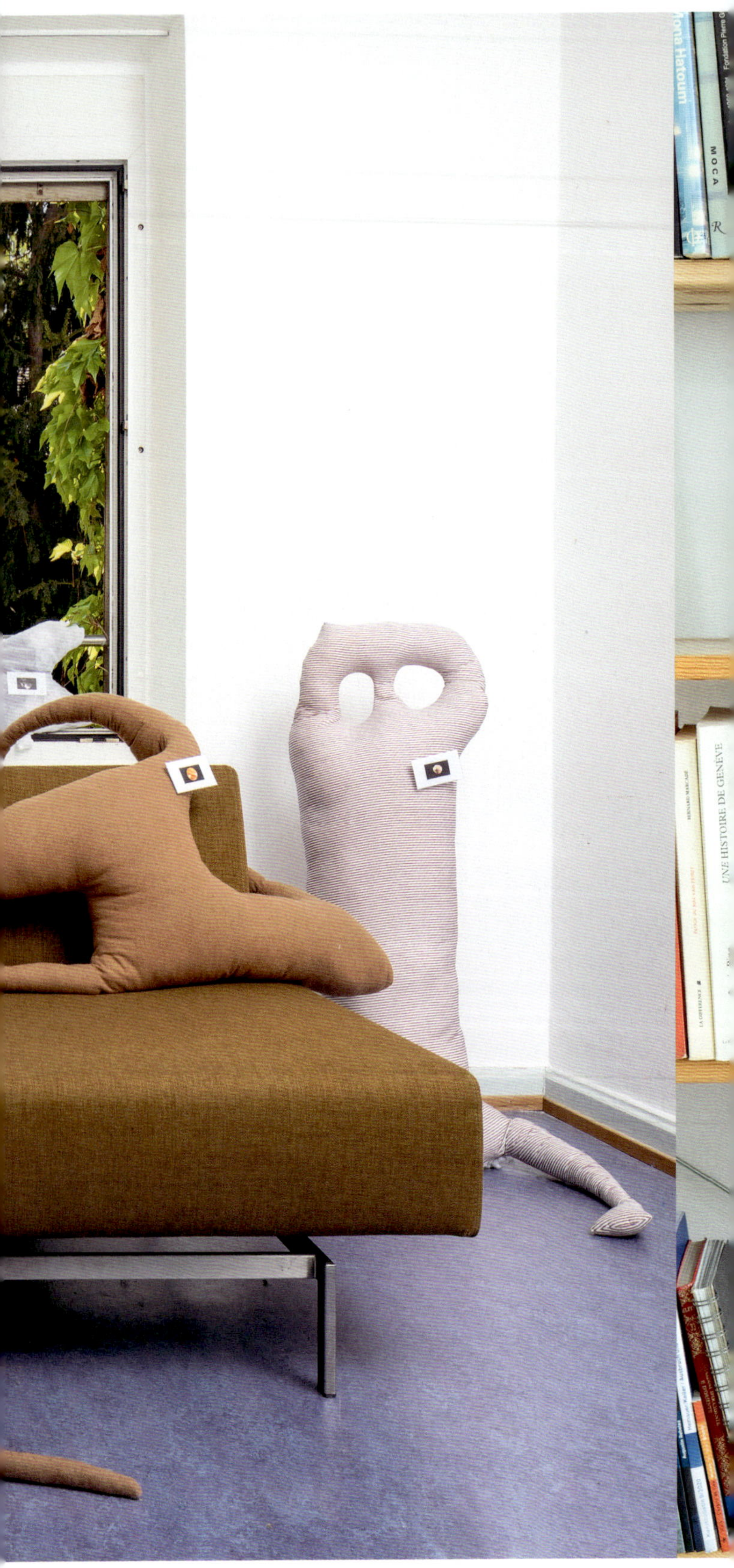

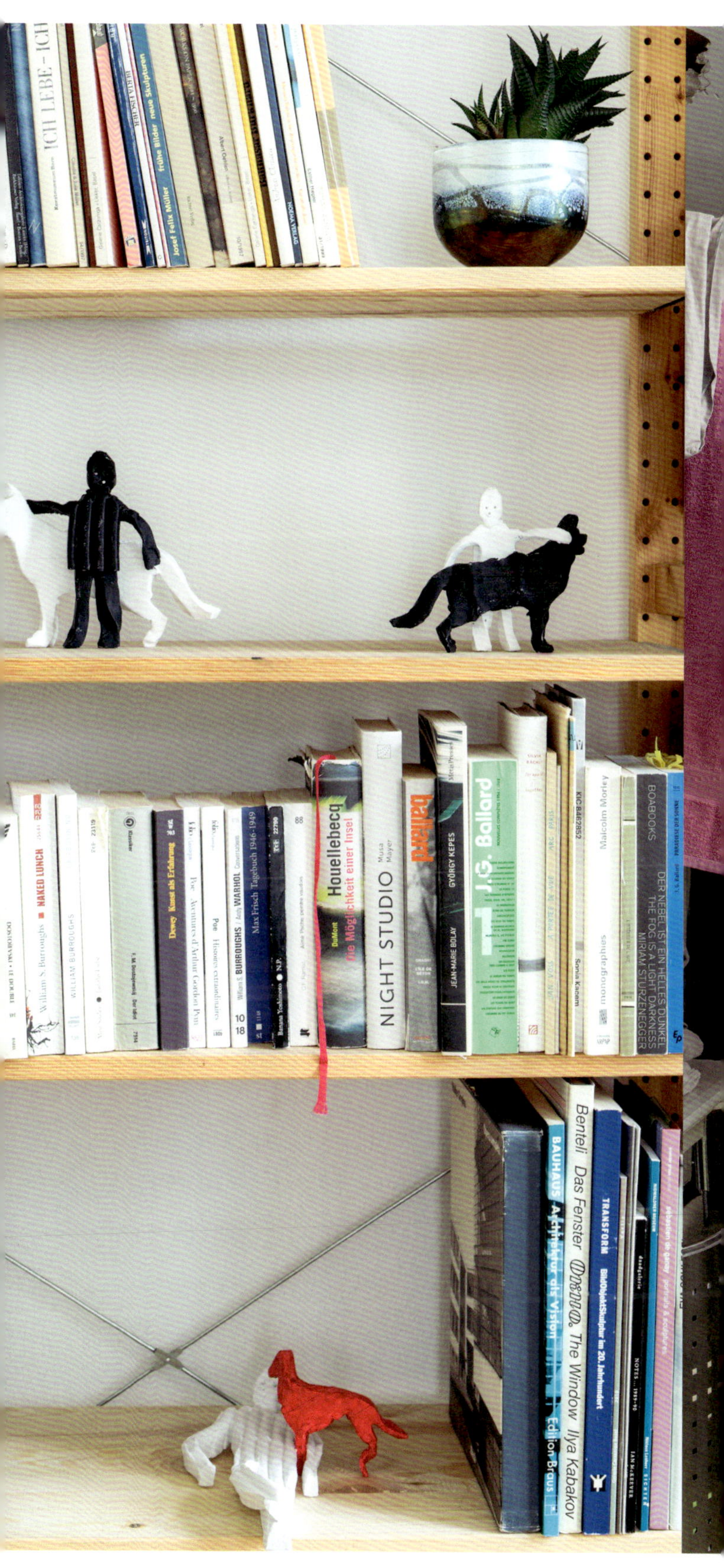

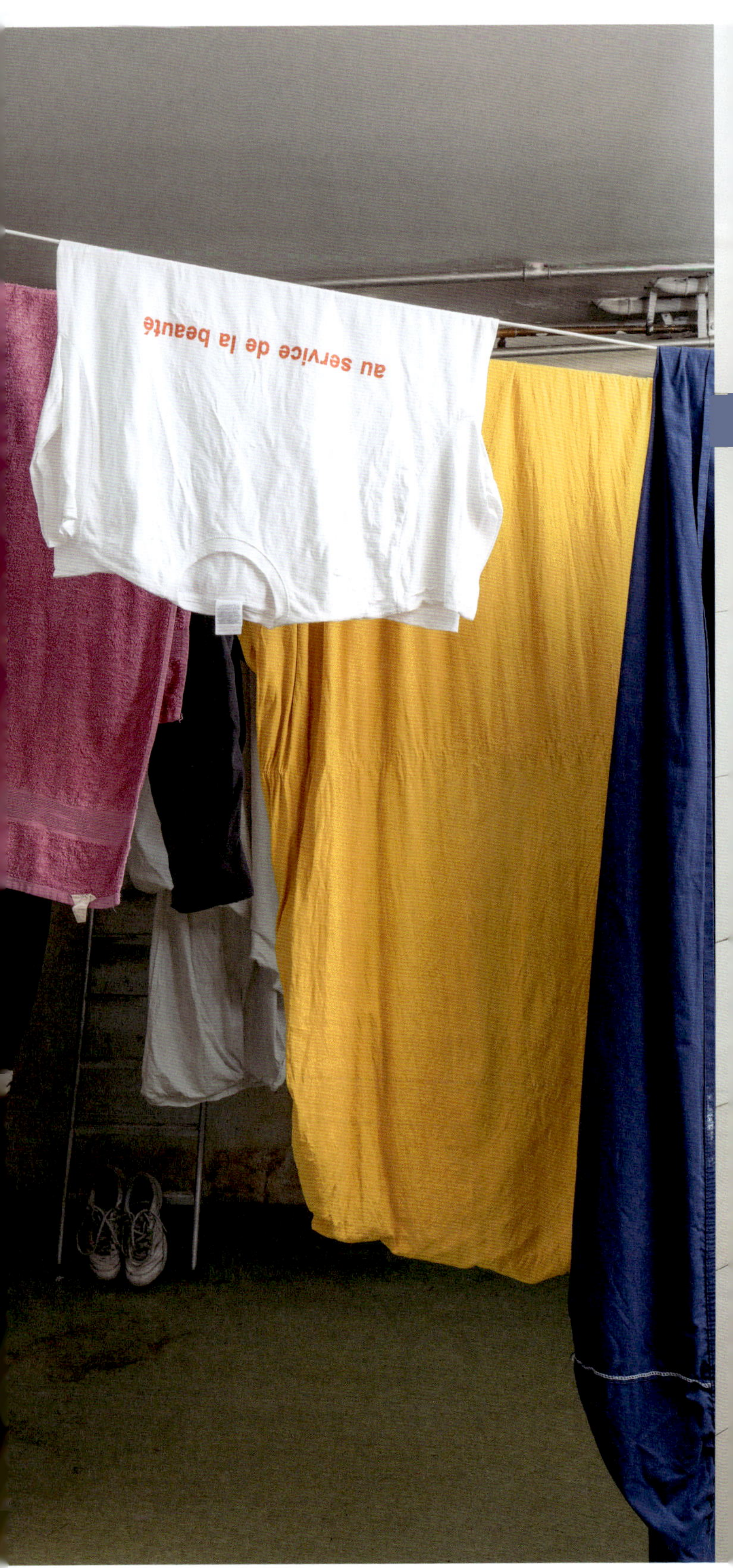
au service de la beauté

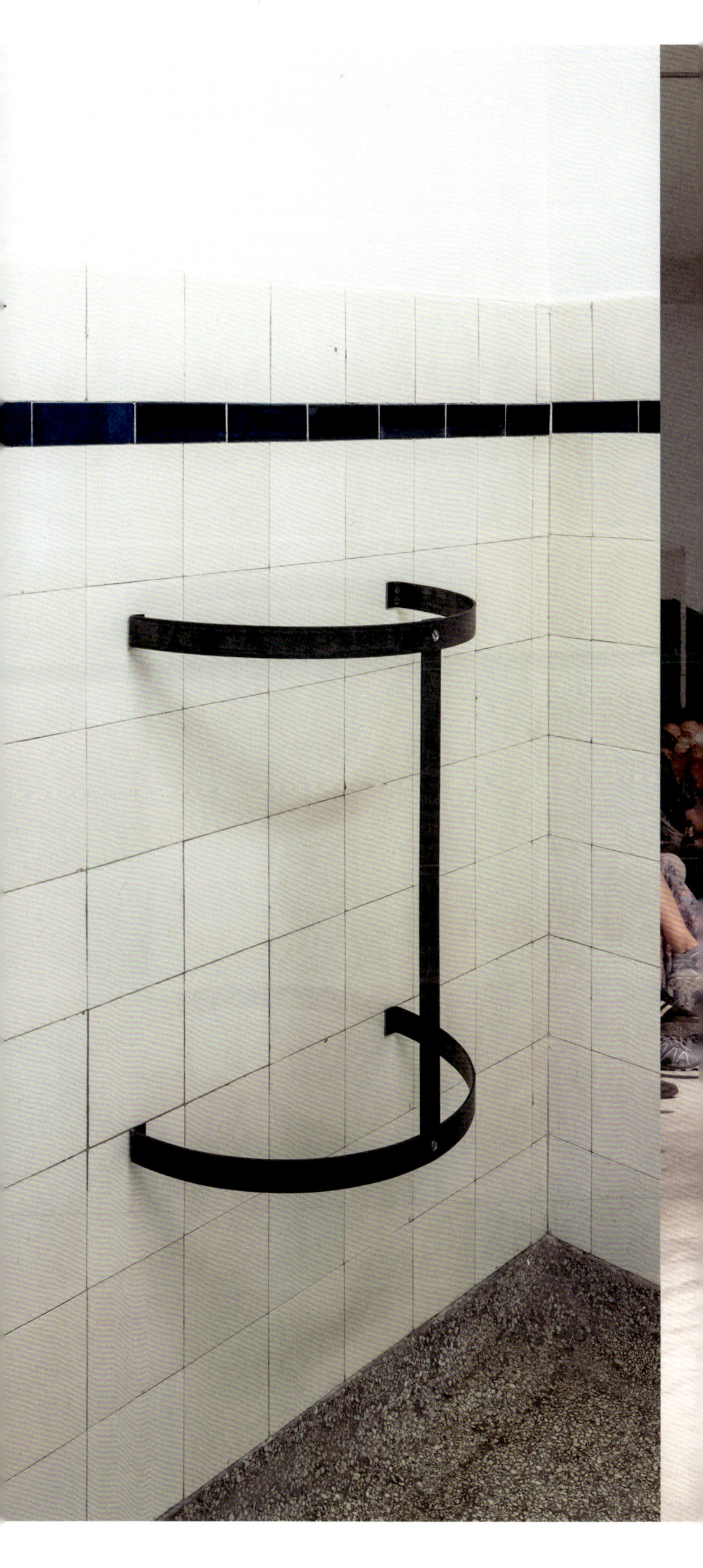

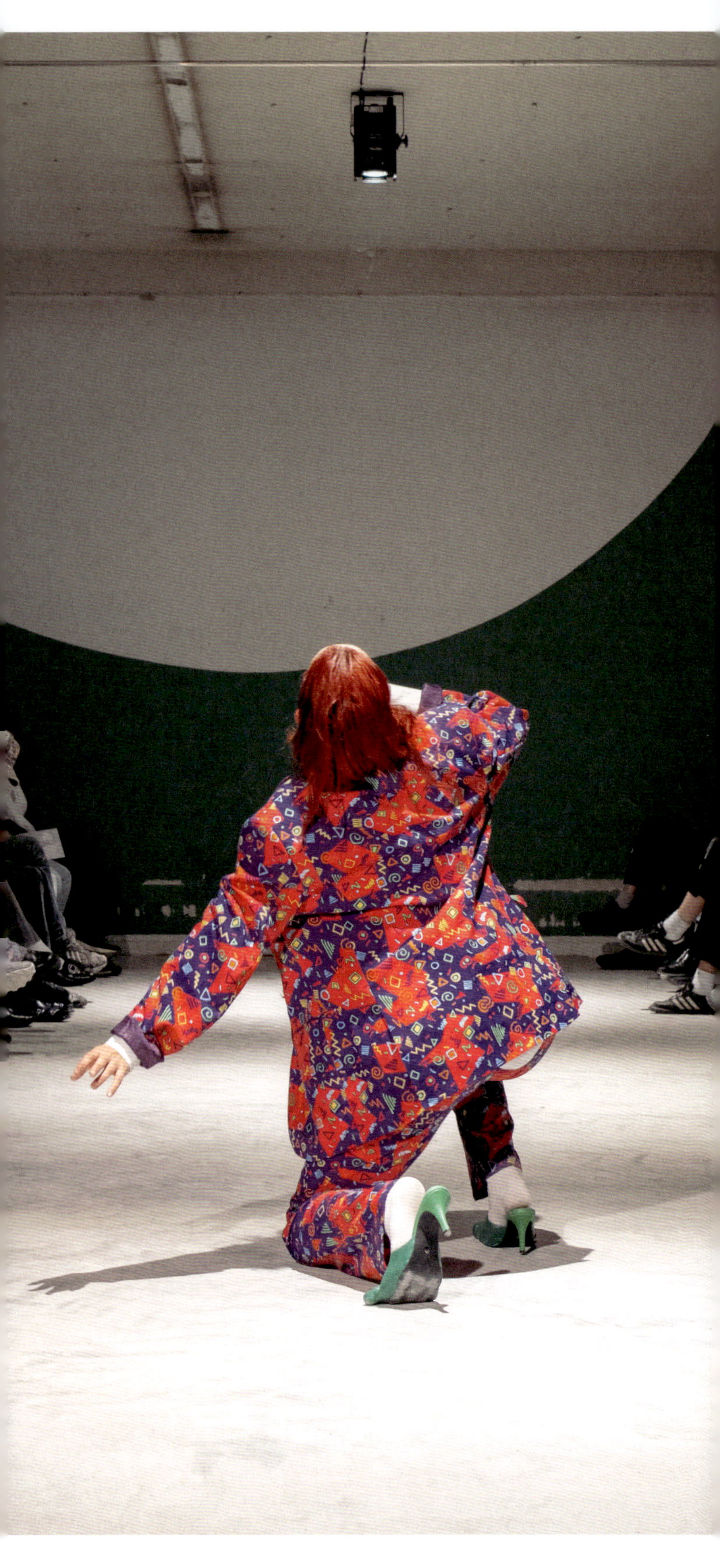

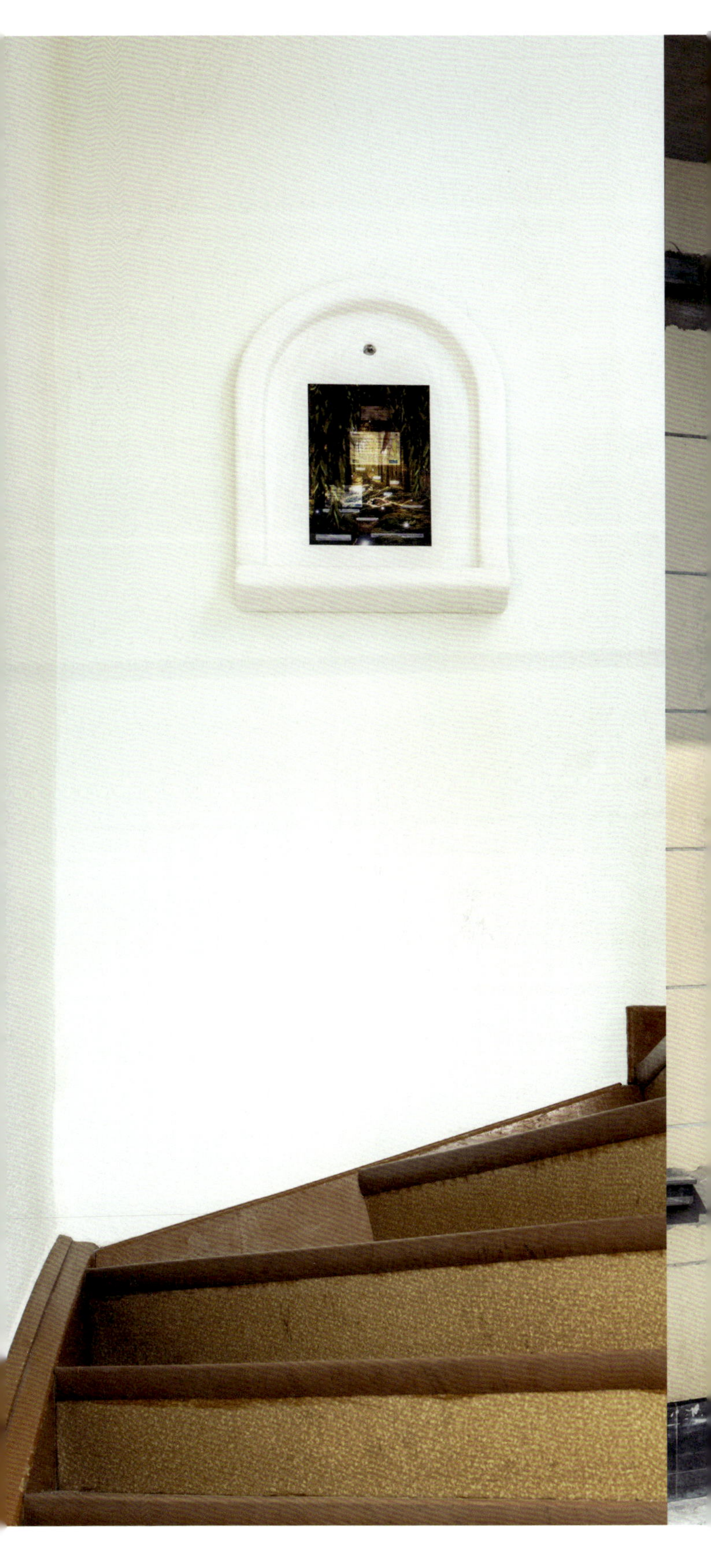

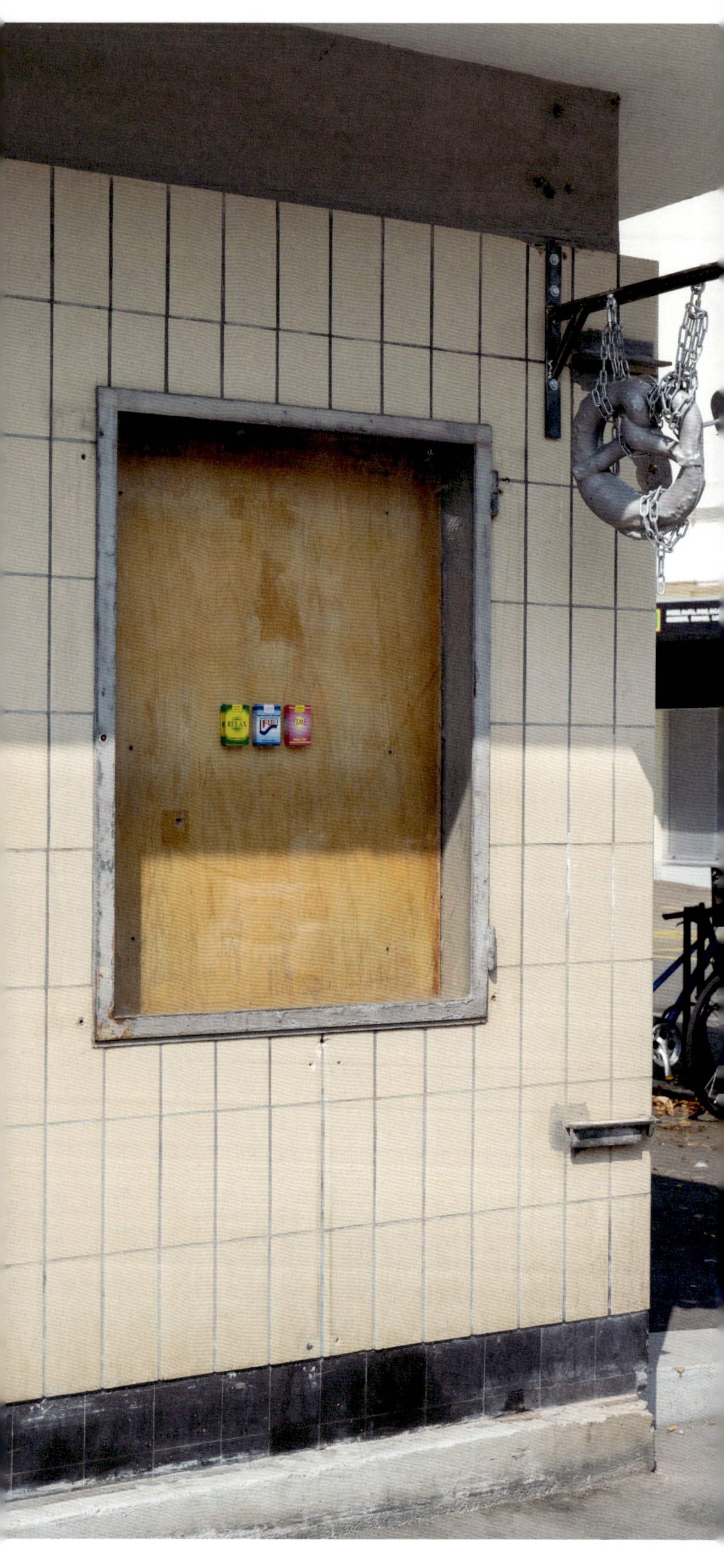

RELAX
FUN
TIME

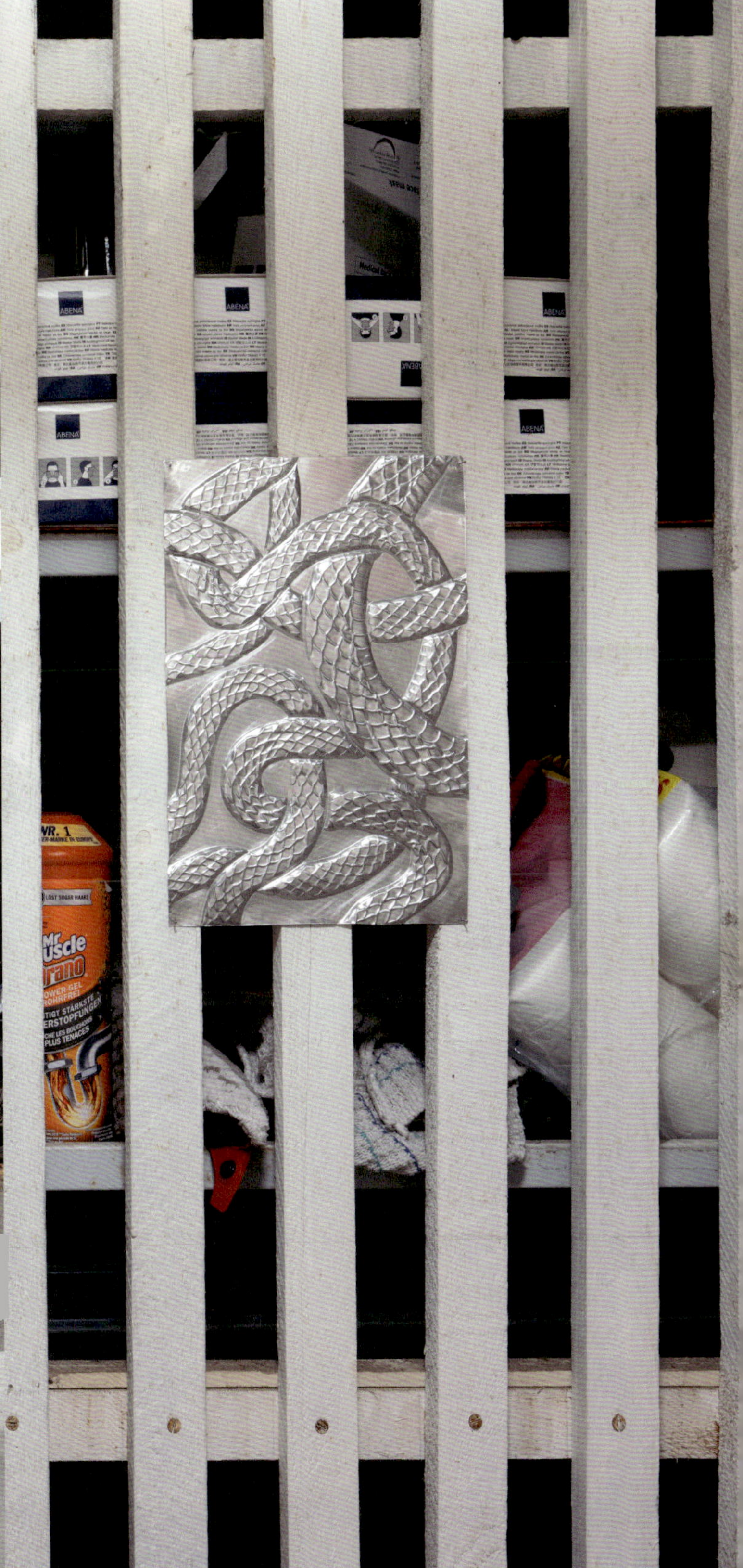

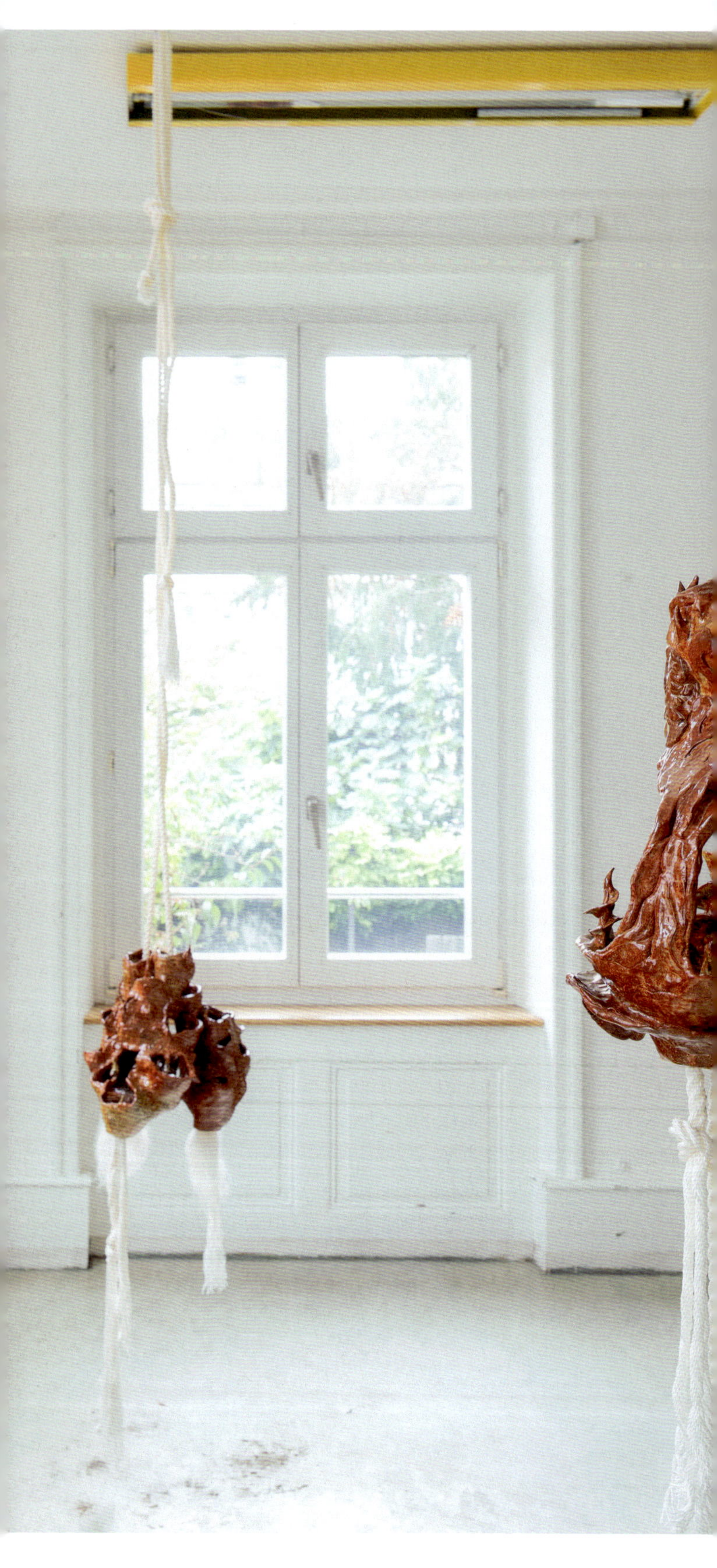

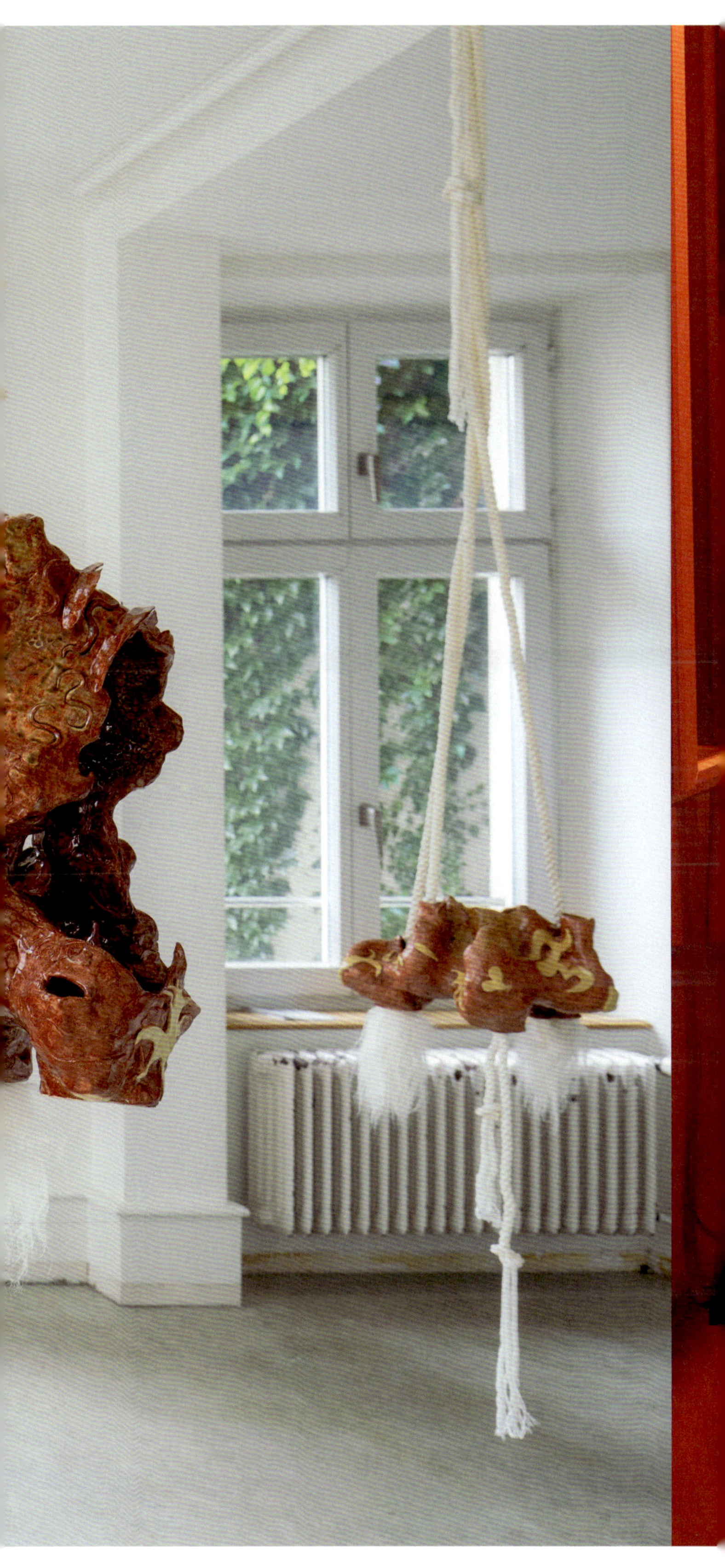

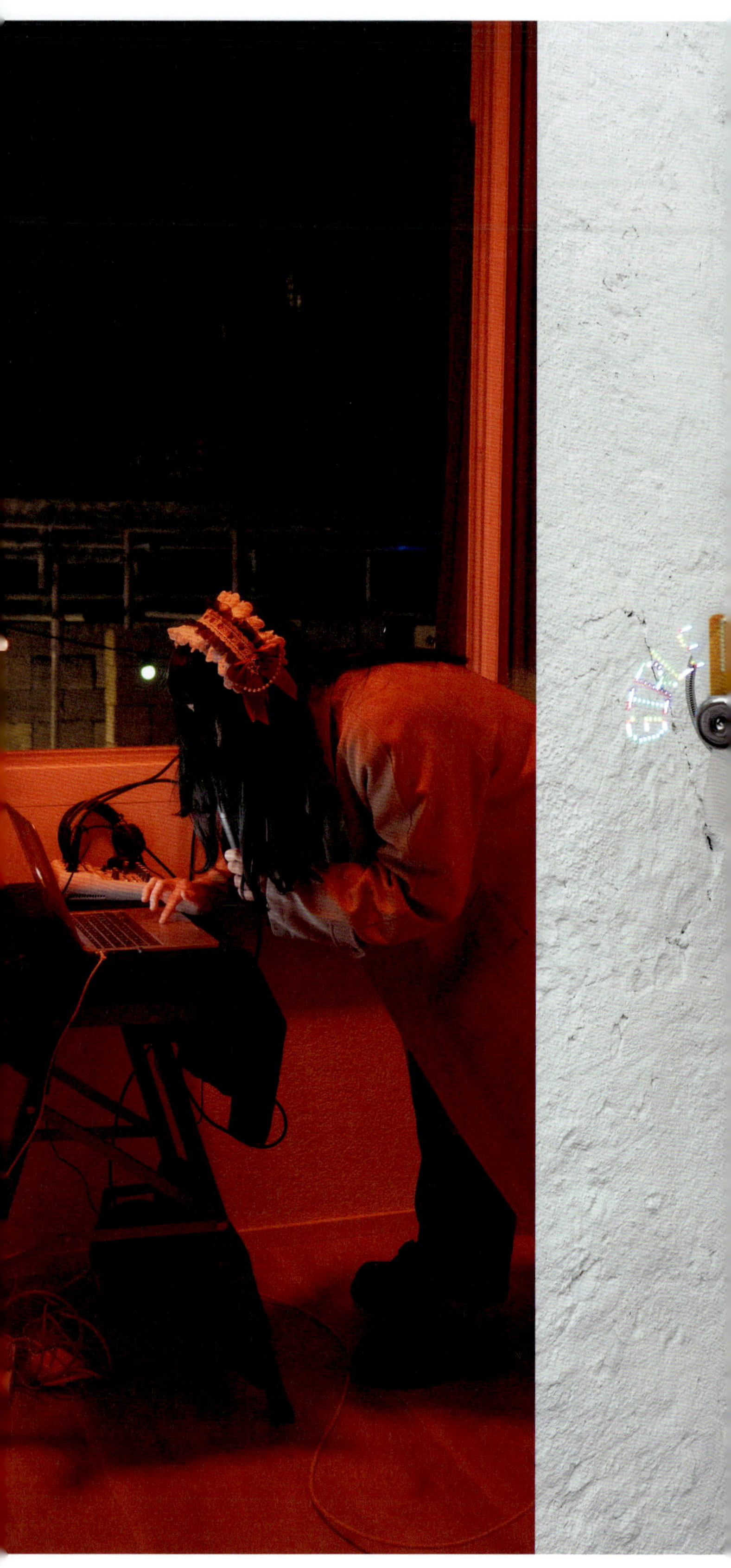

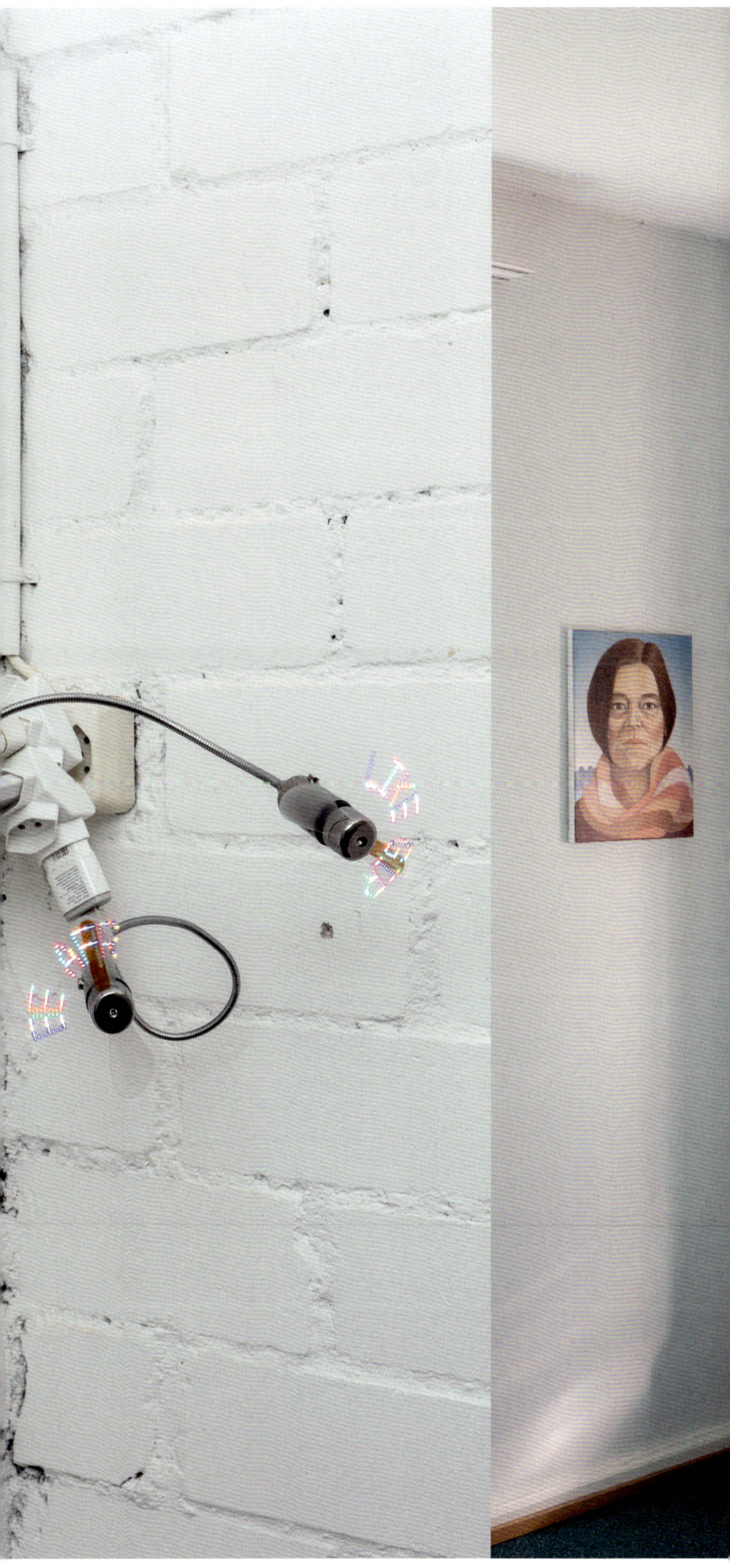

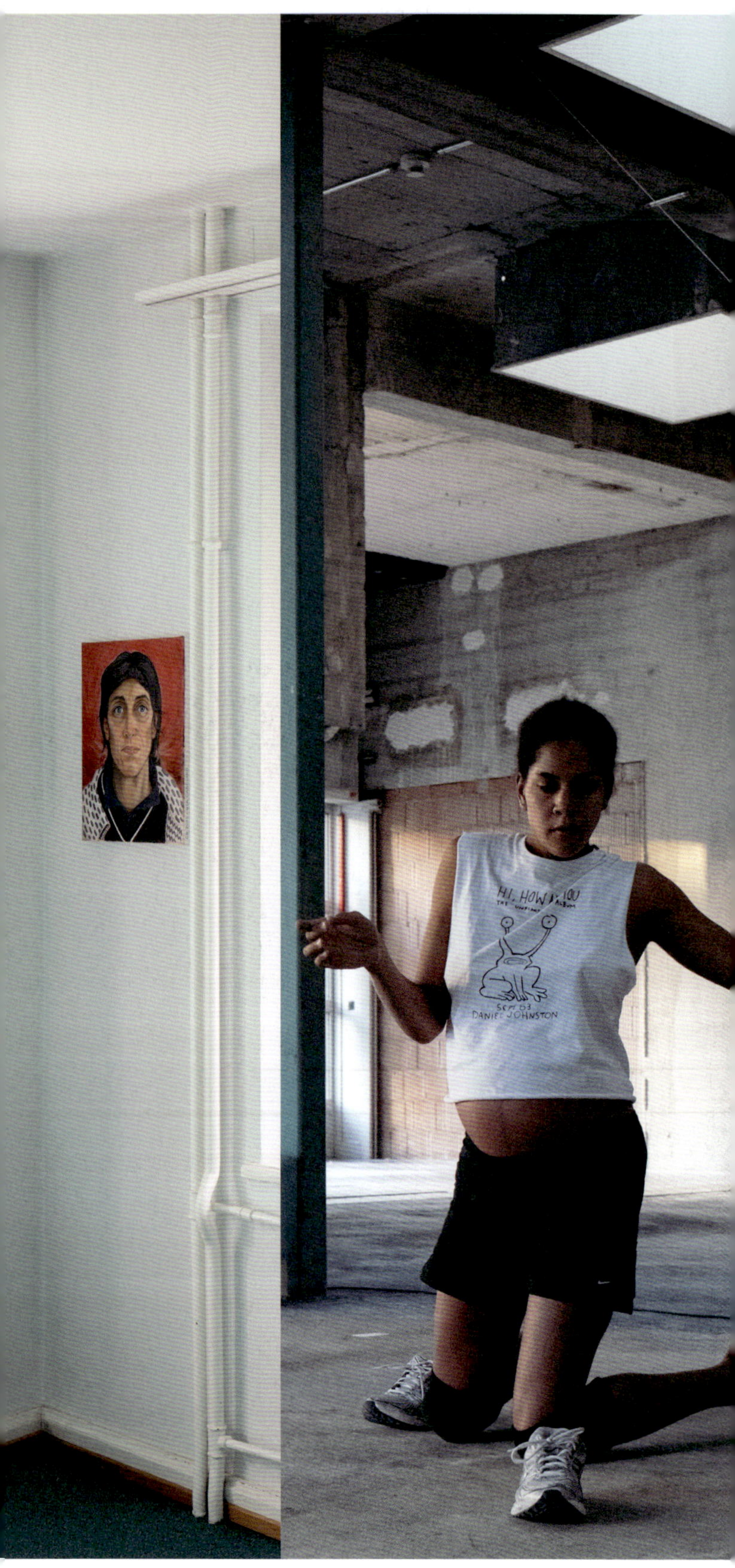

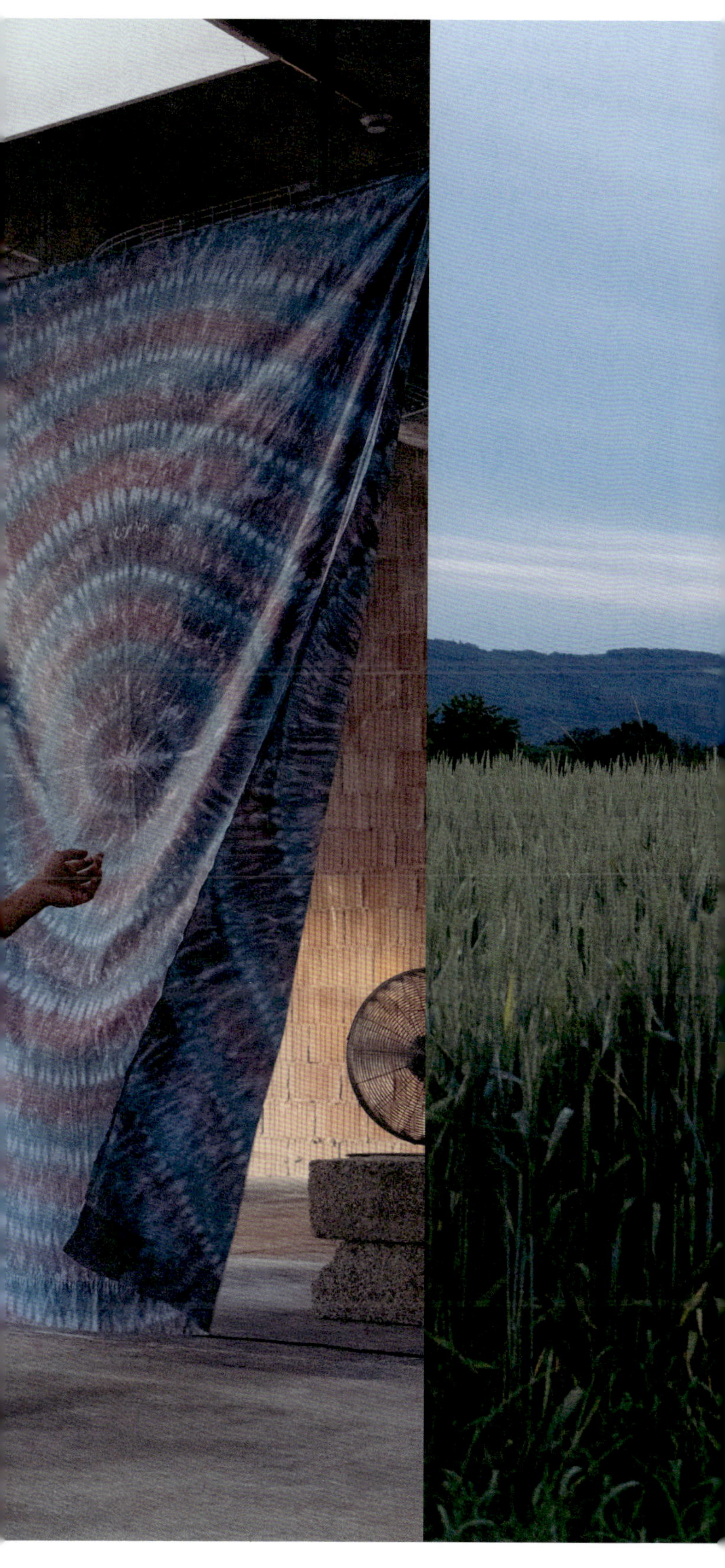

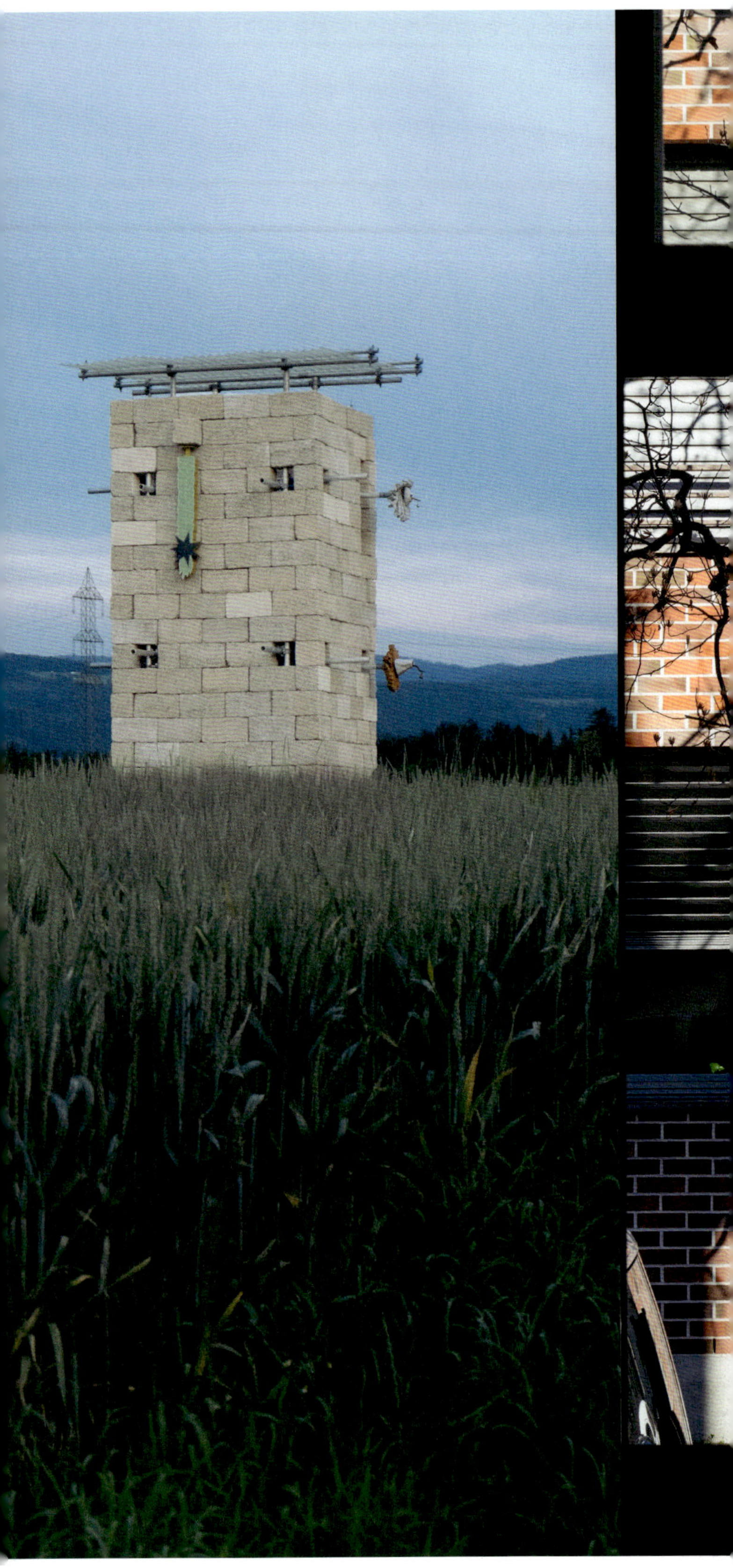

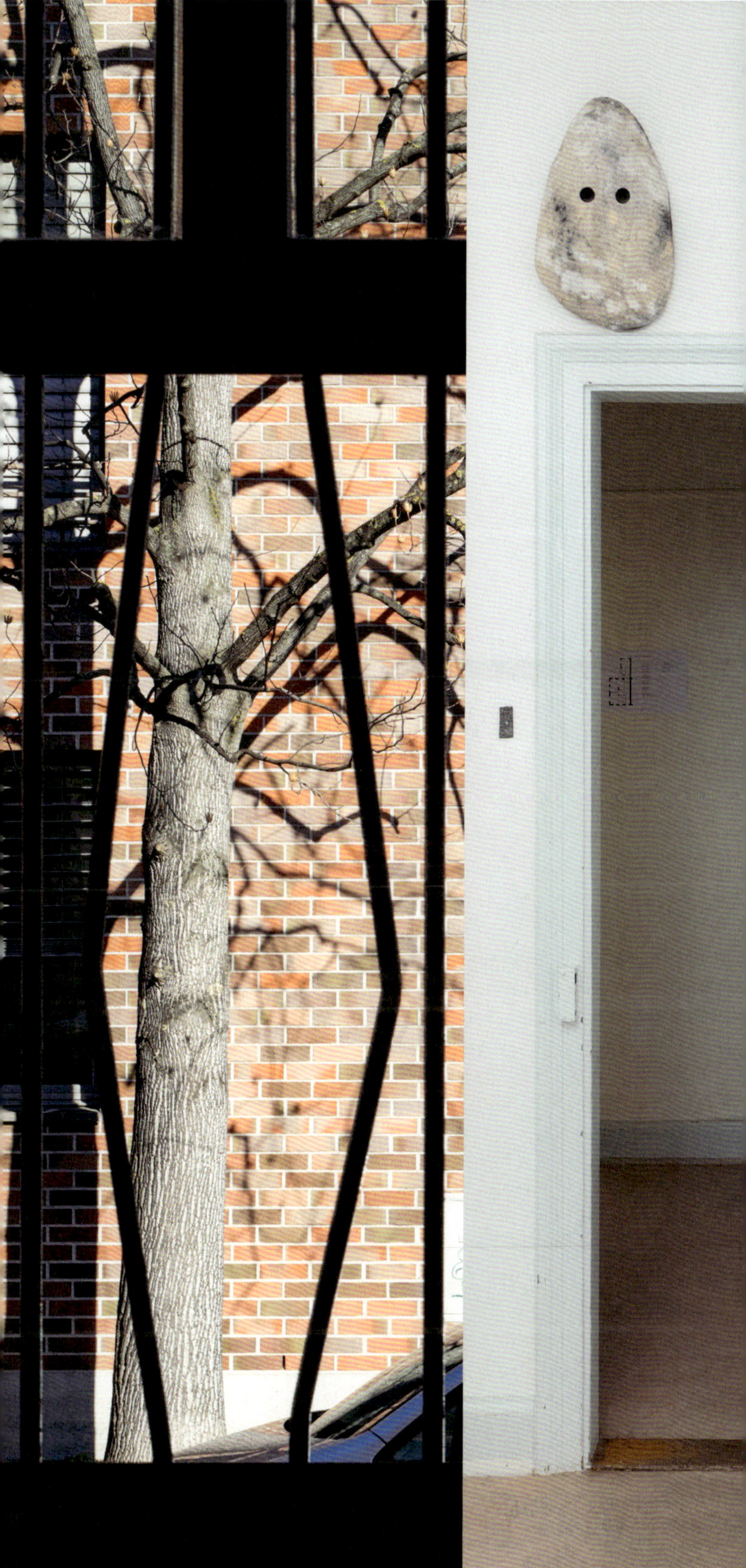

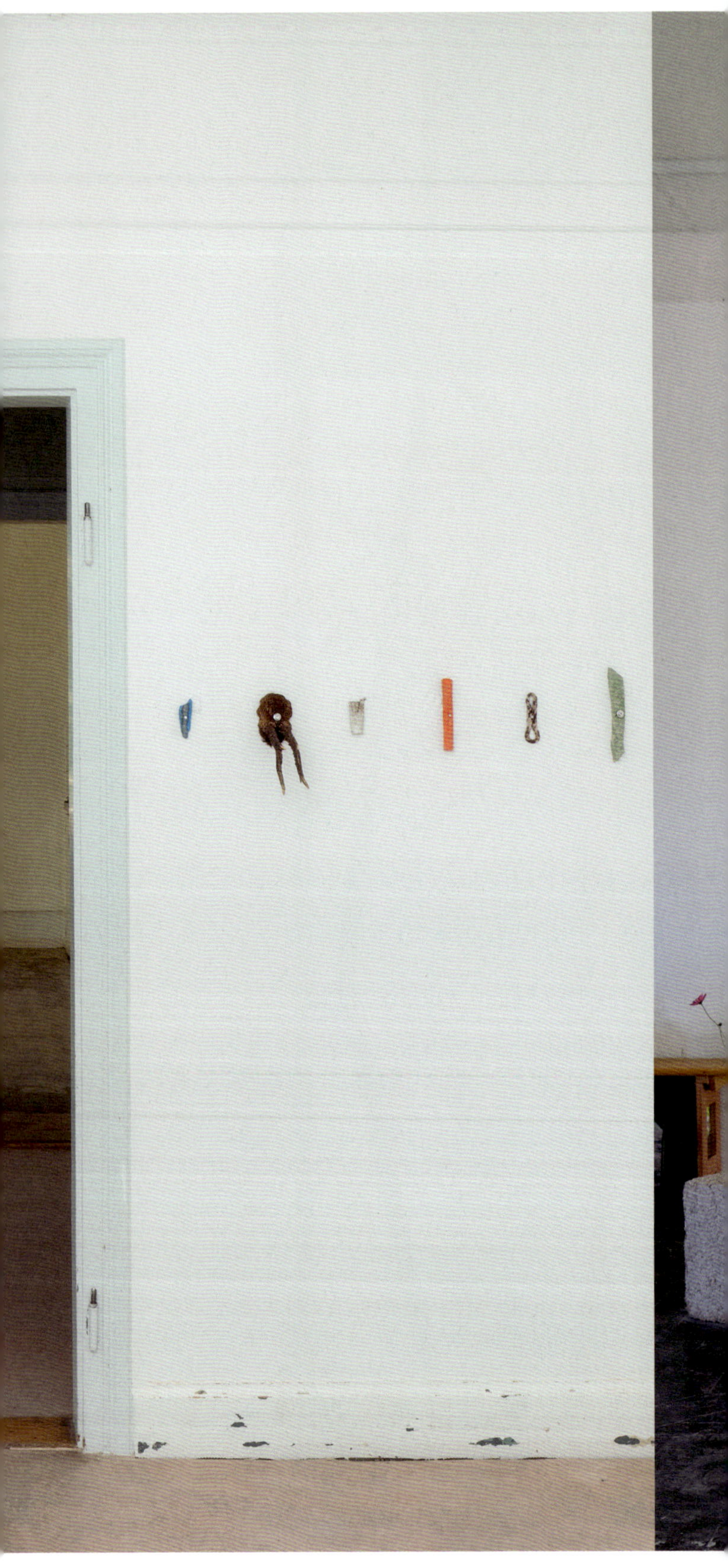

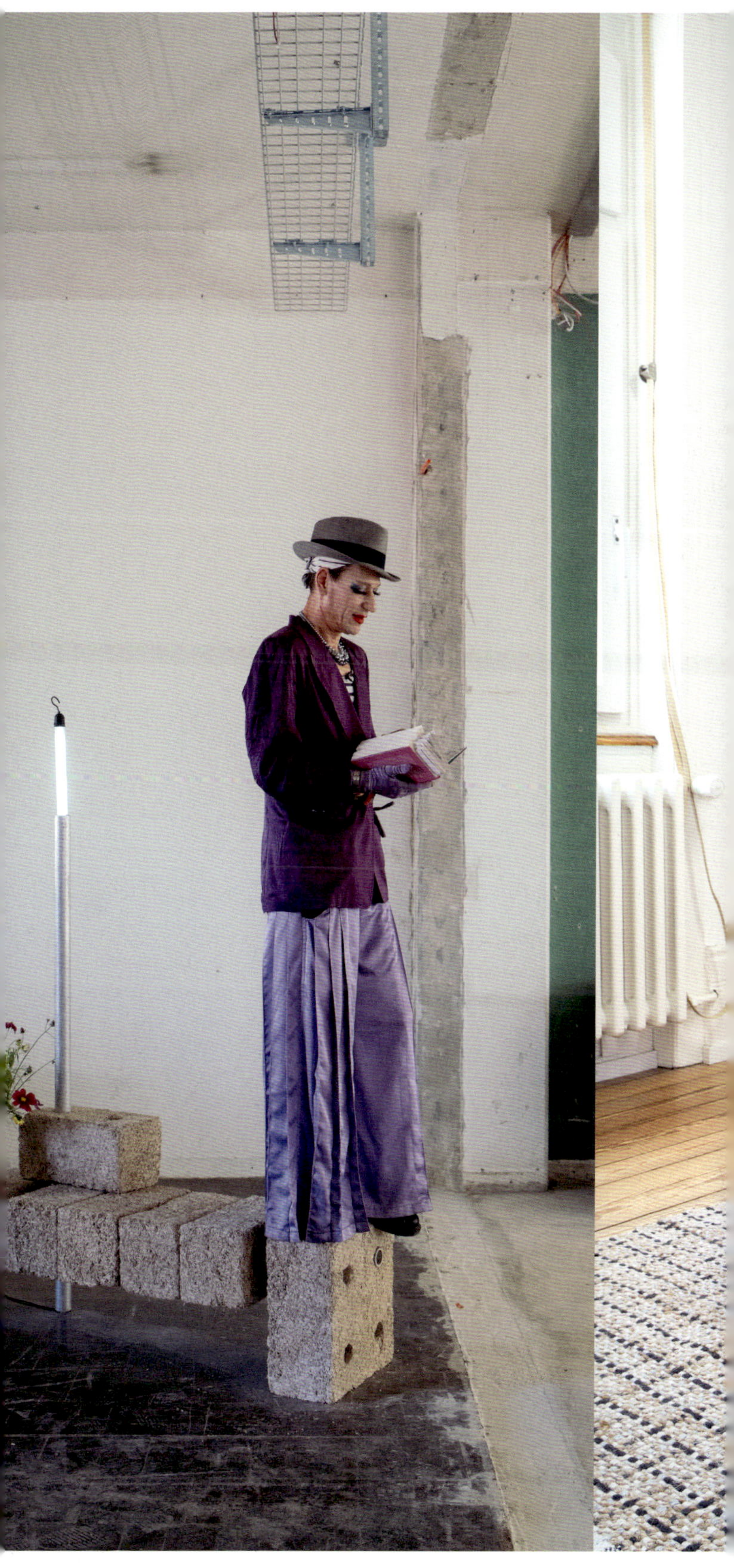

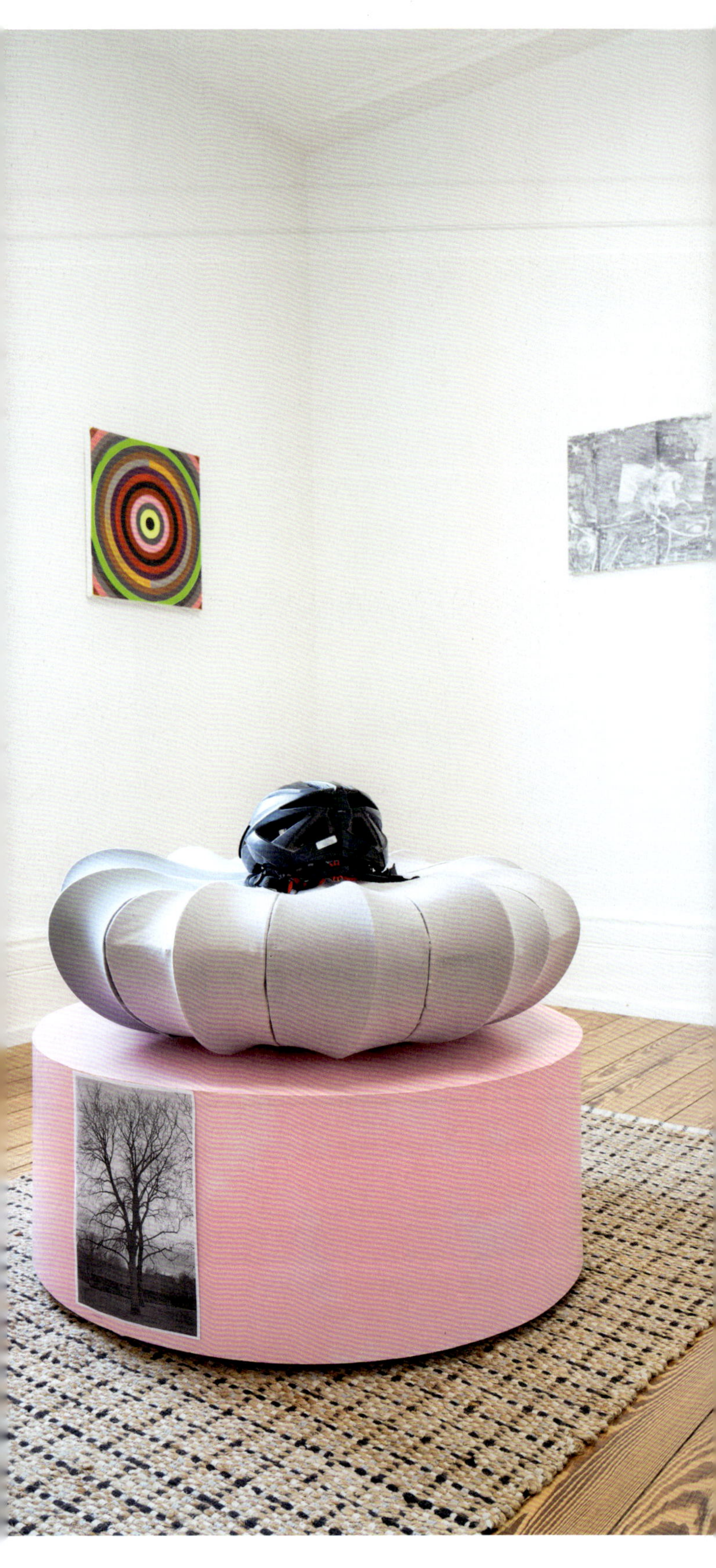

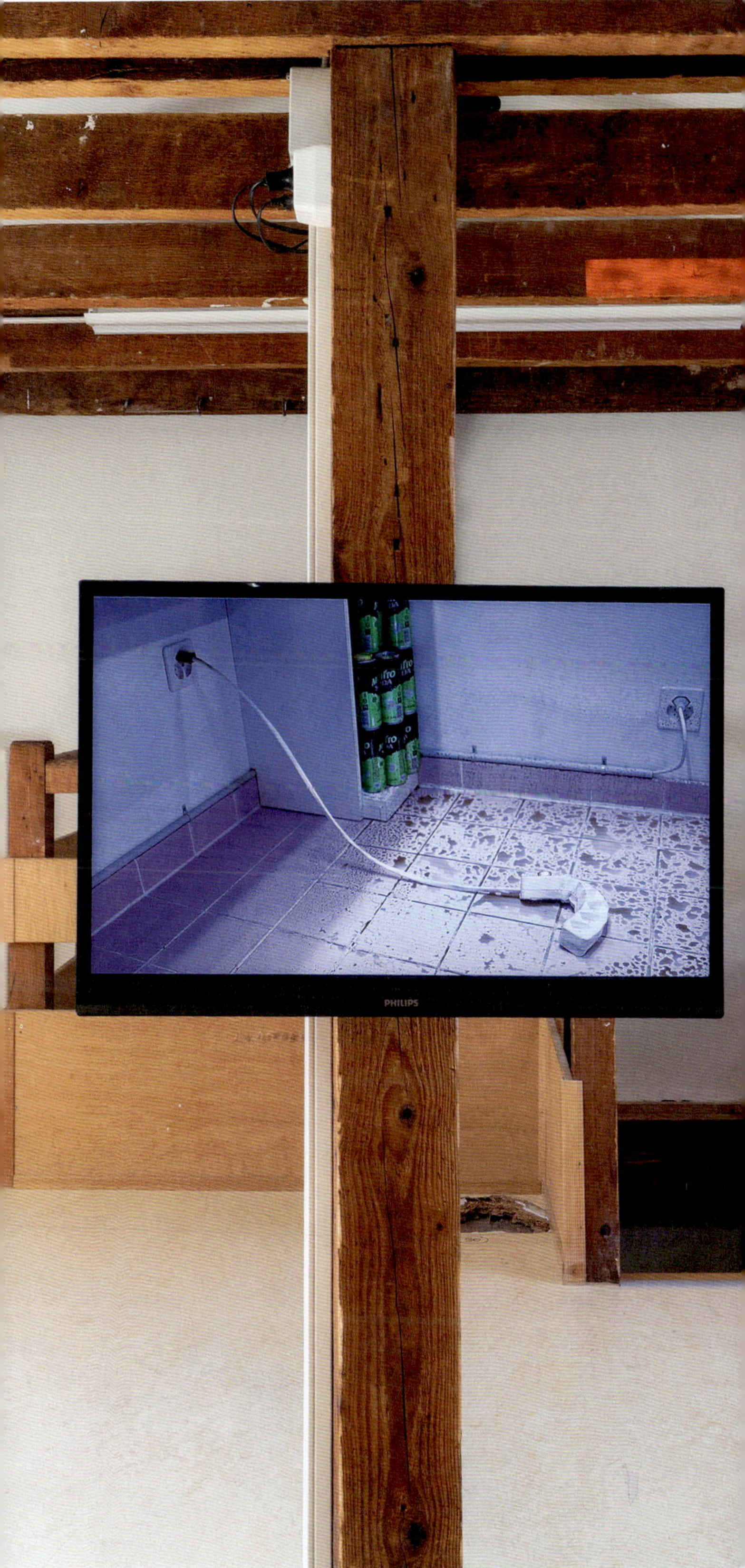

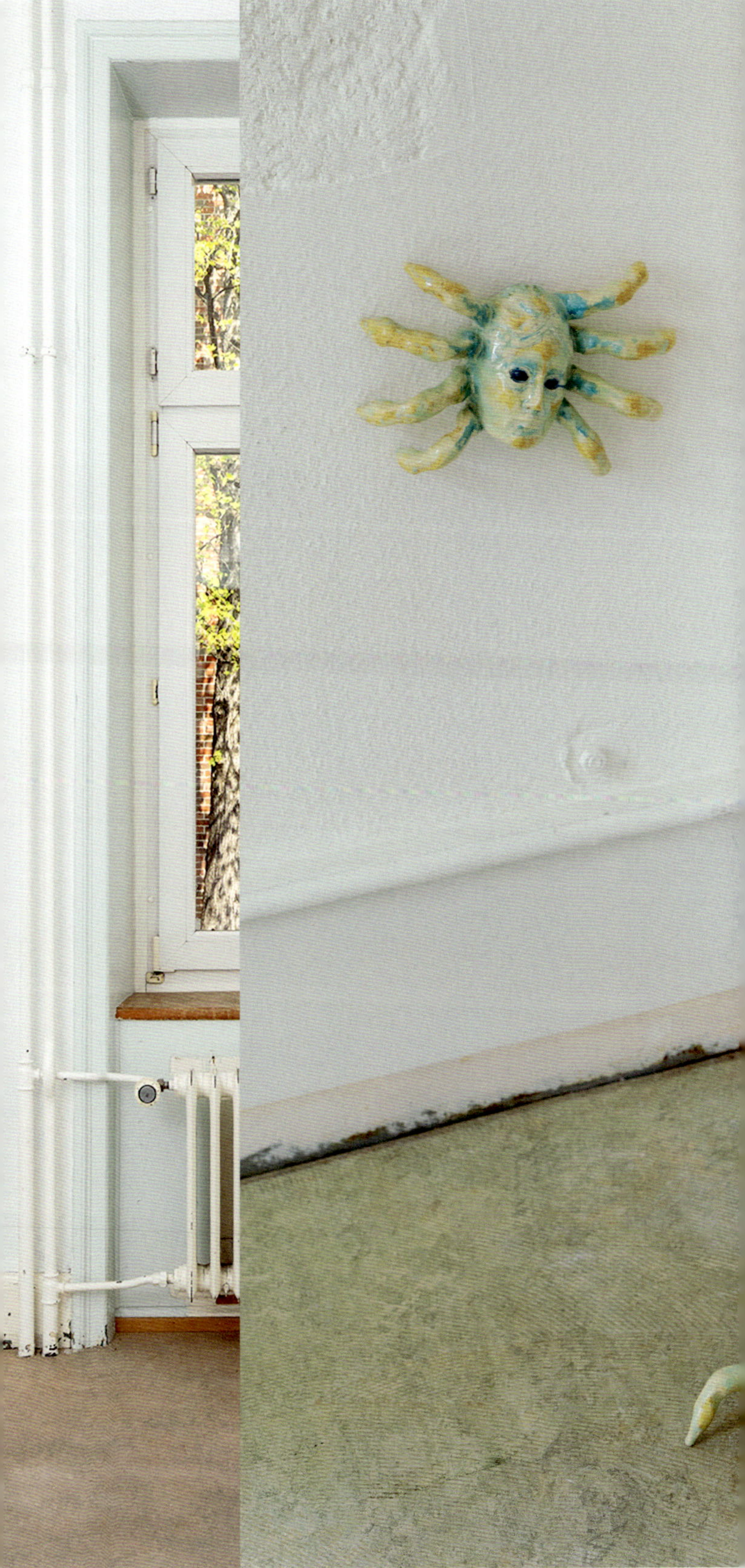

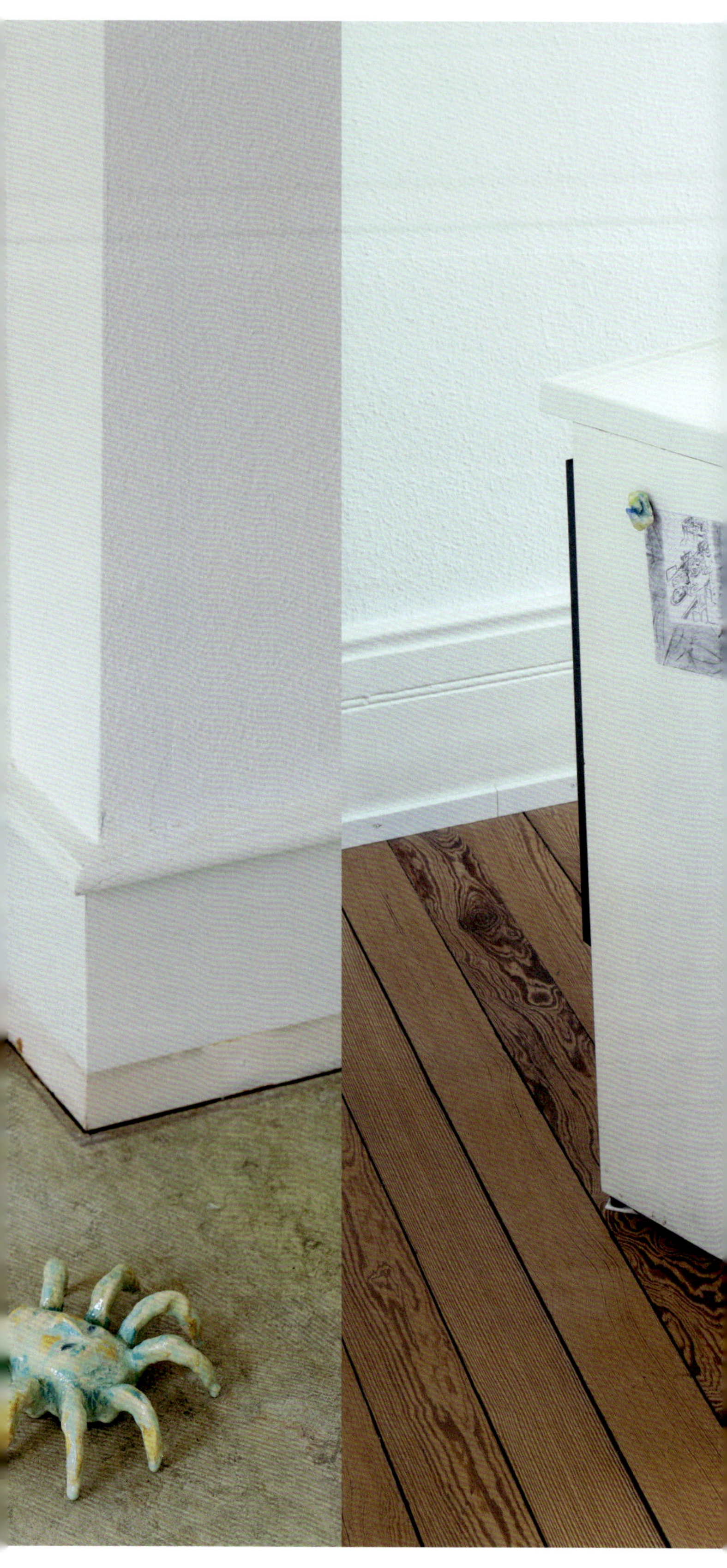

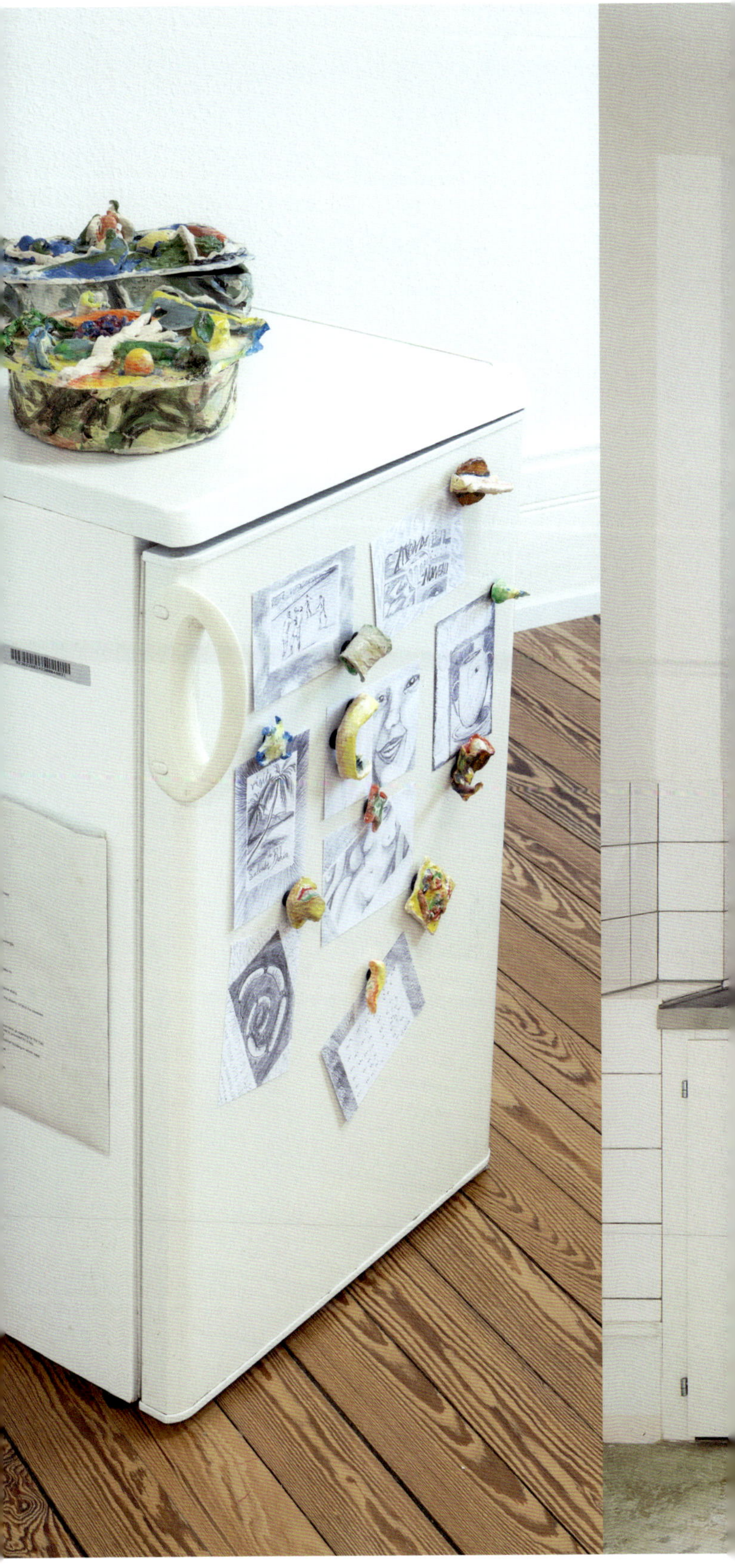

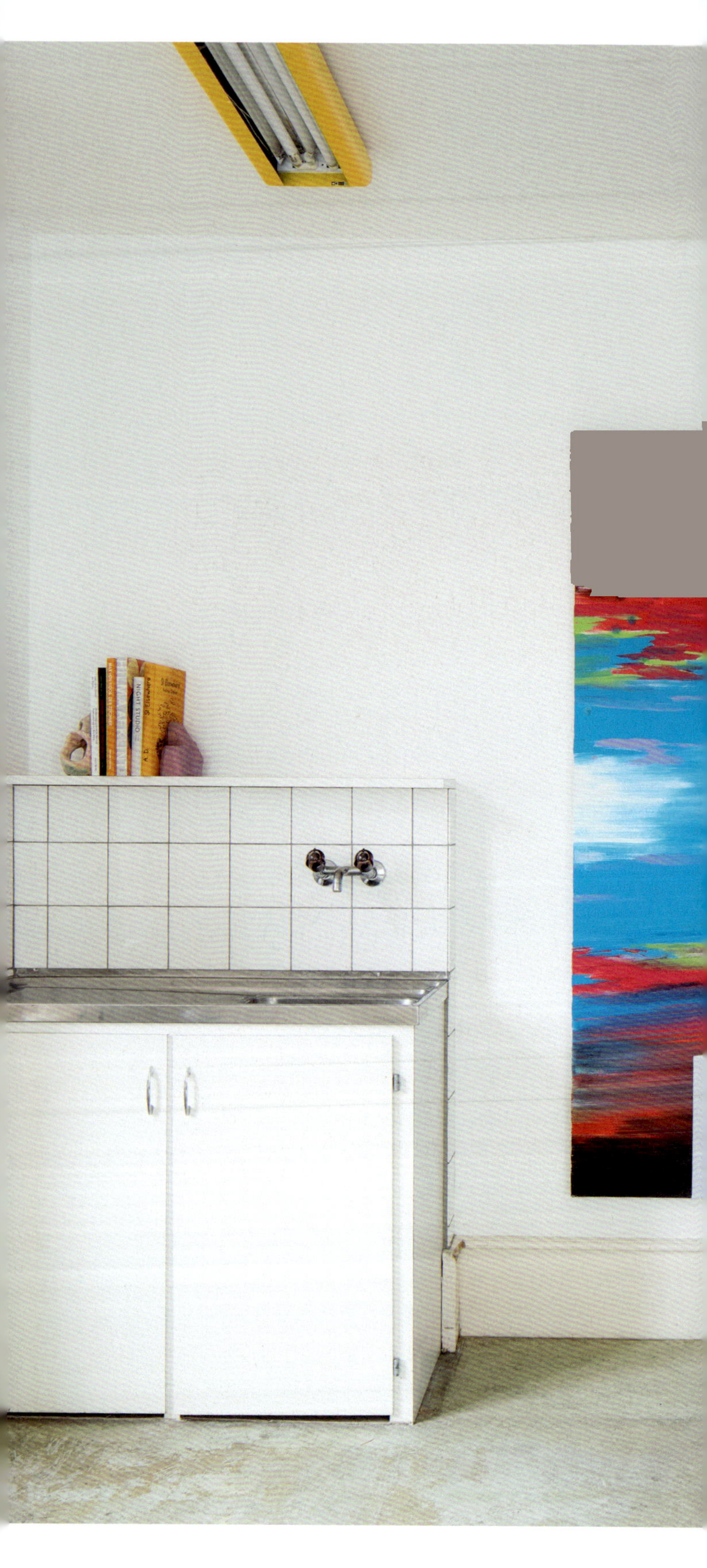

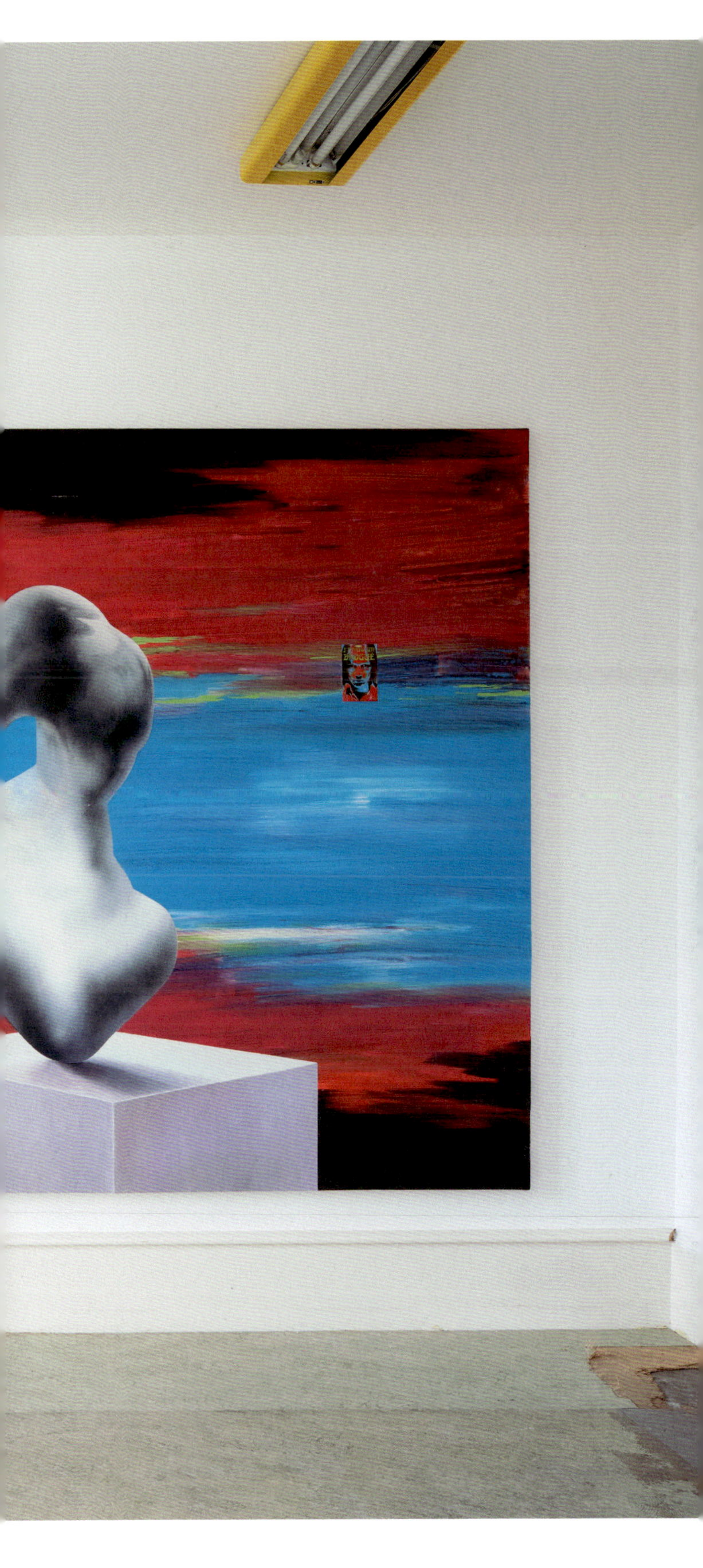

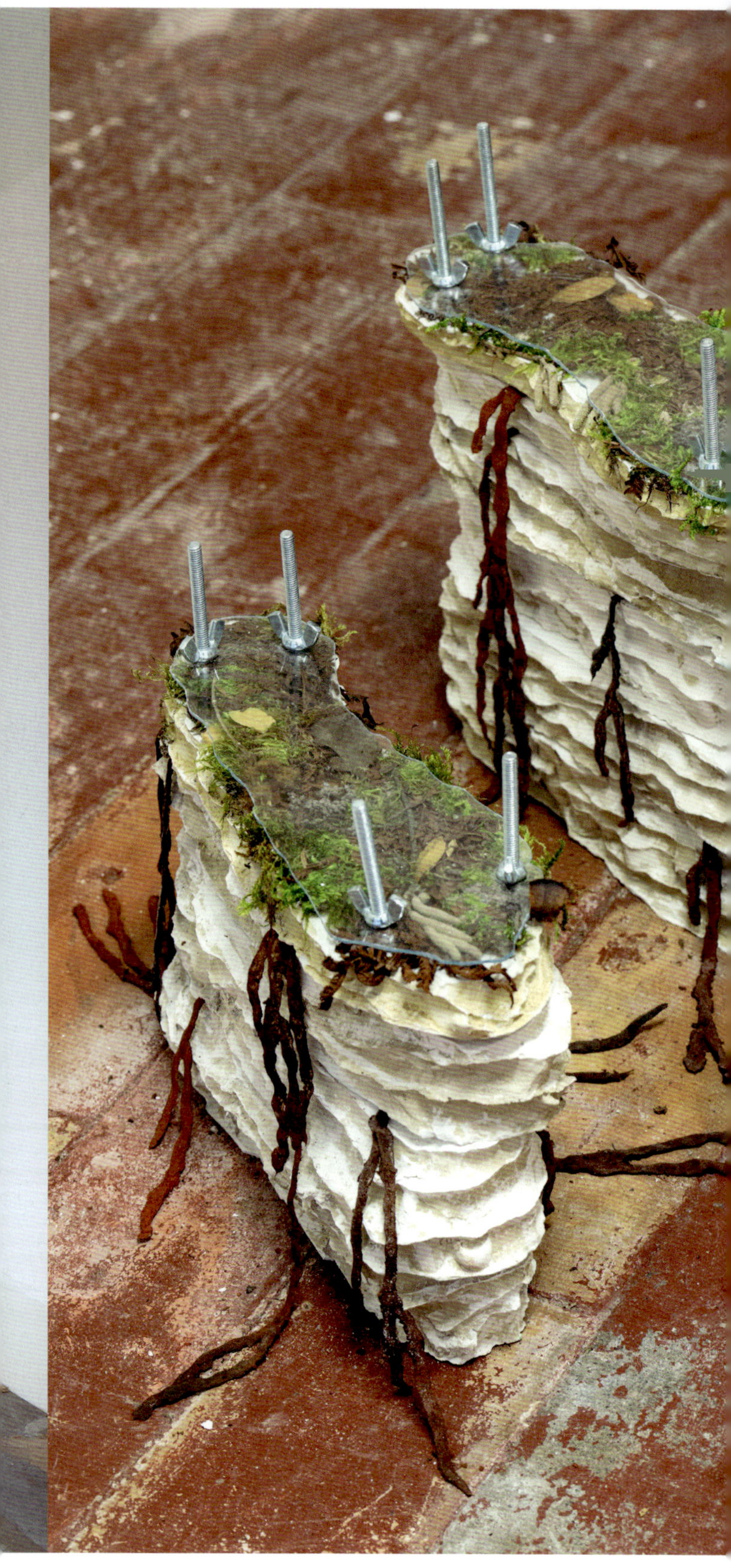

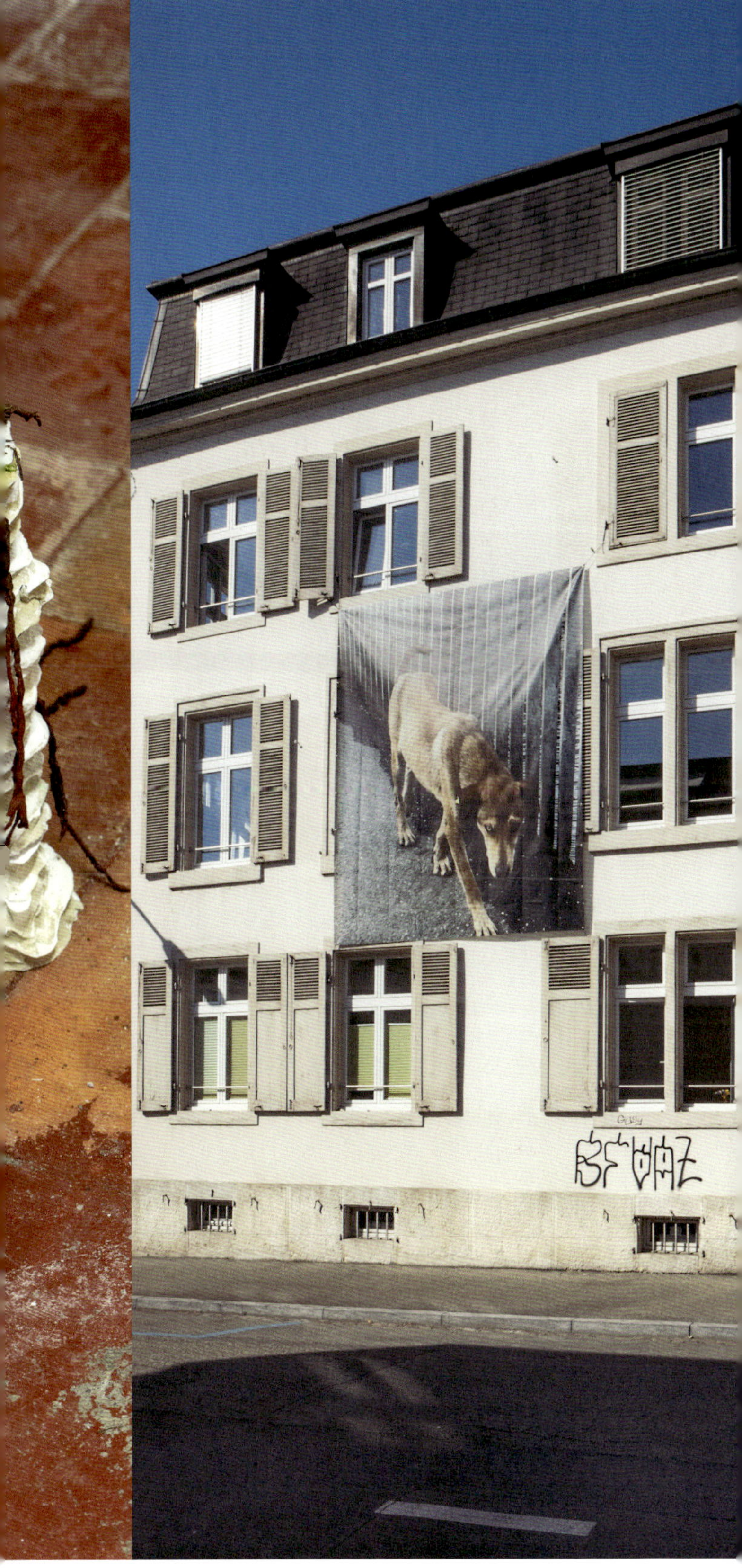

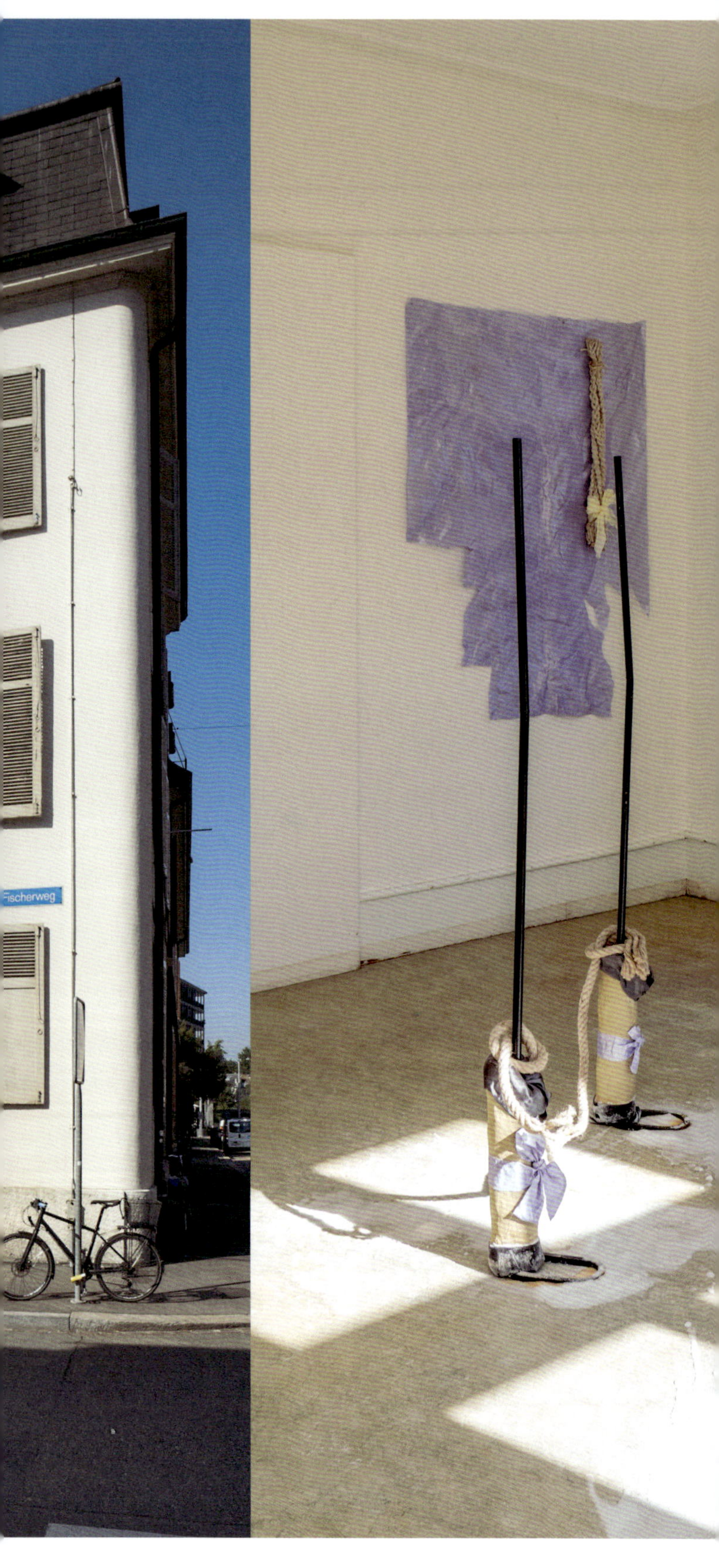
Fischerweg

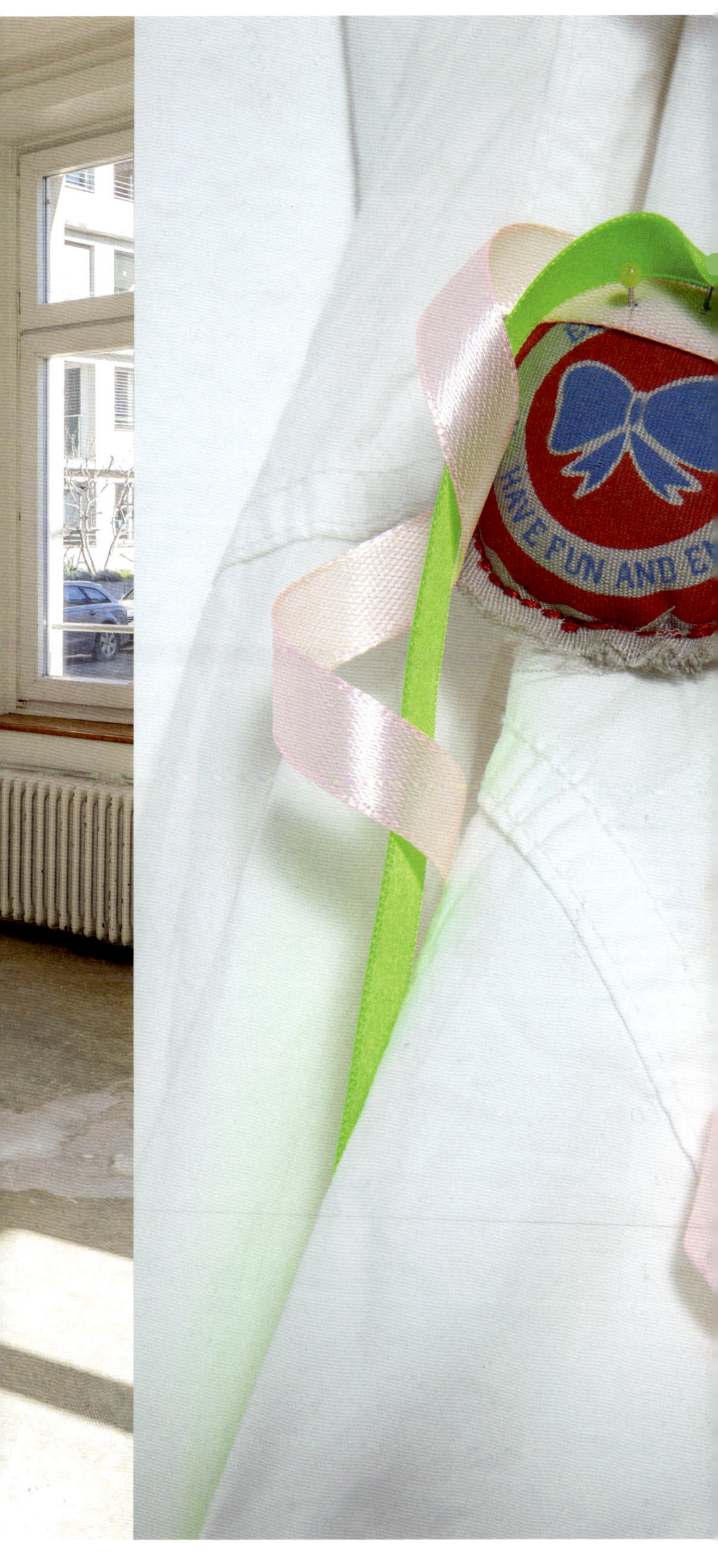
HAVE FUN AND EN

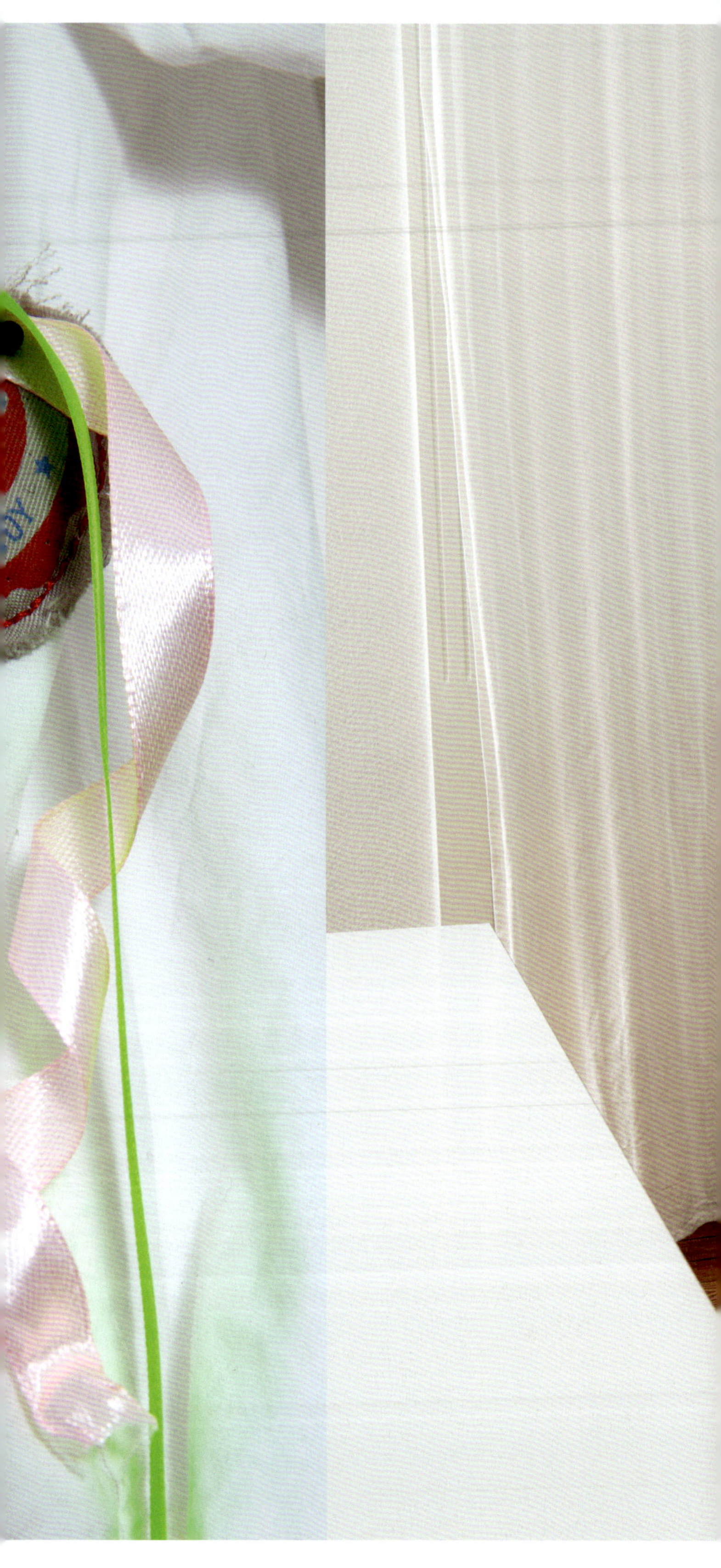

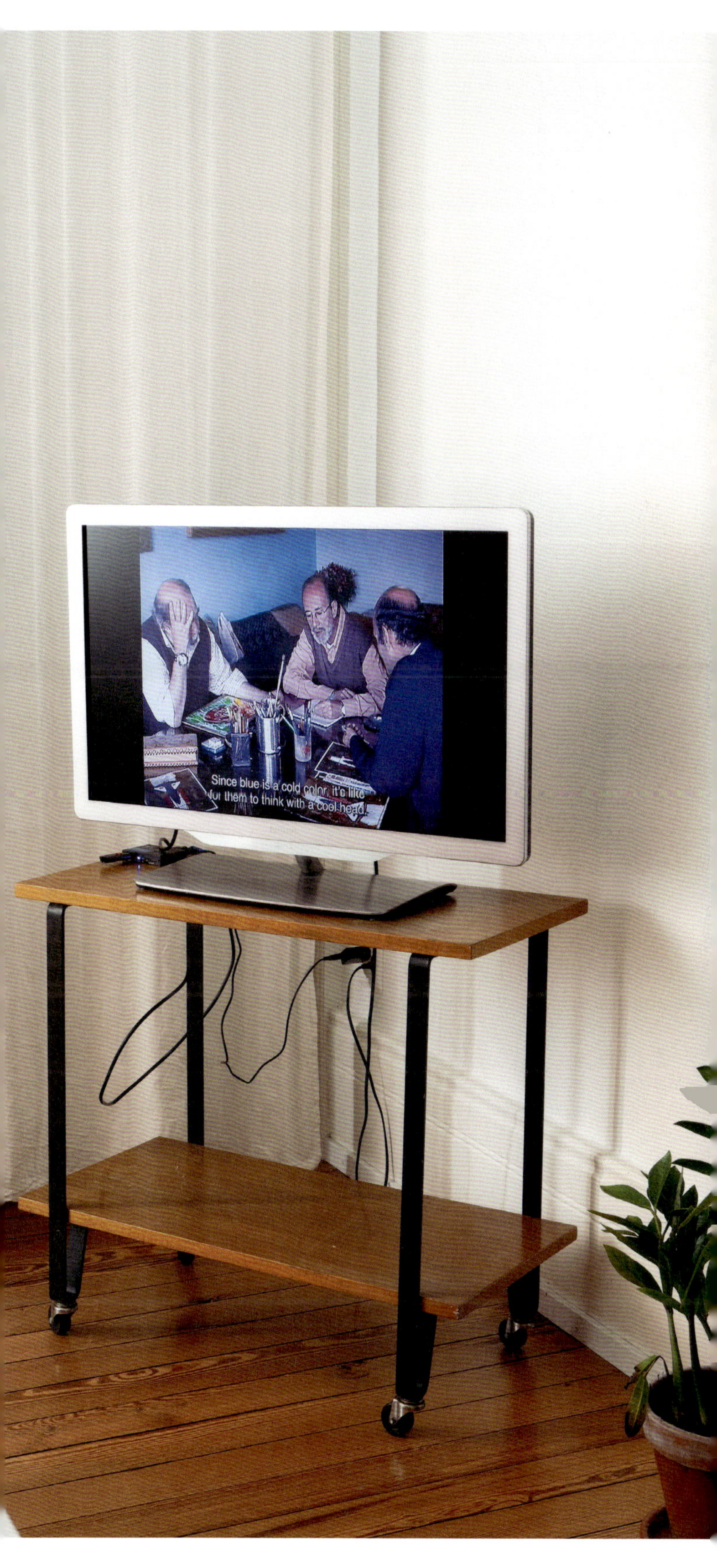
Since blue is a cold color, it's like
for them to think with a cool head!

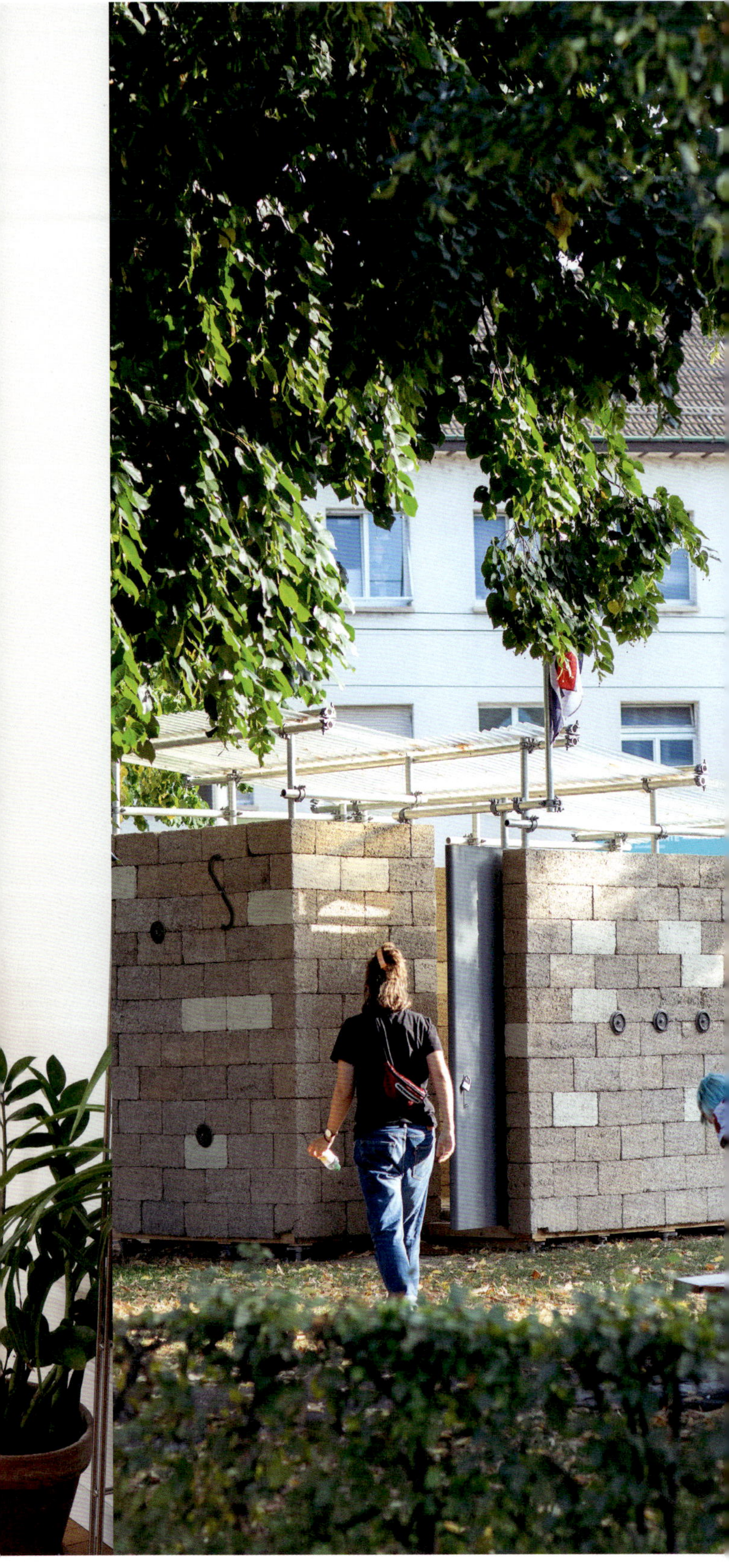

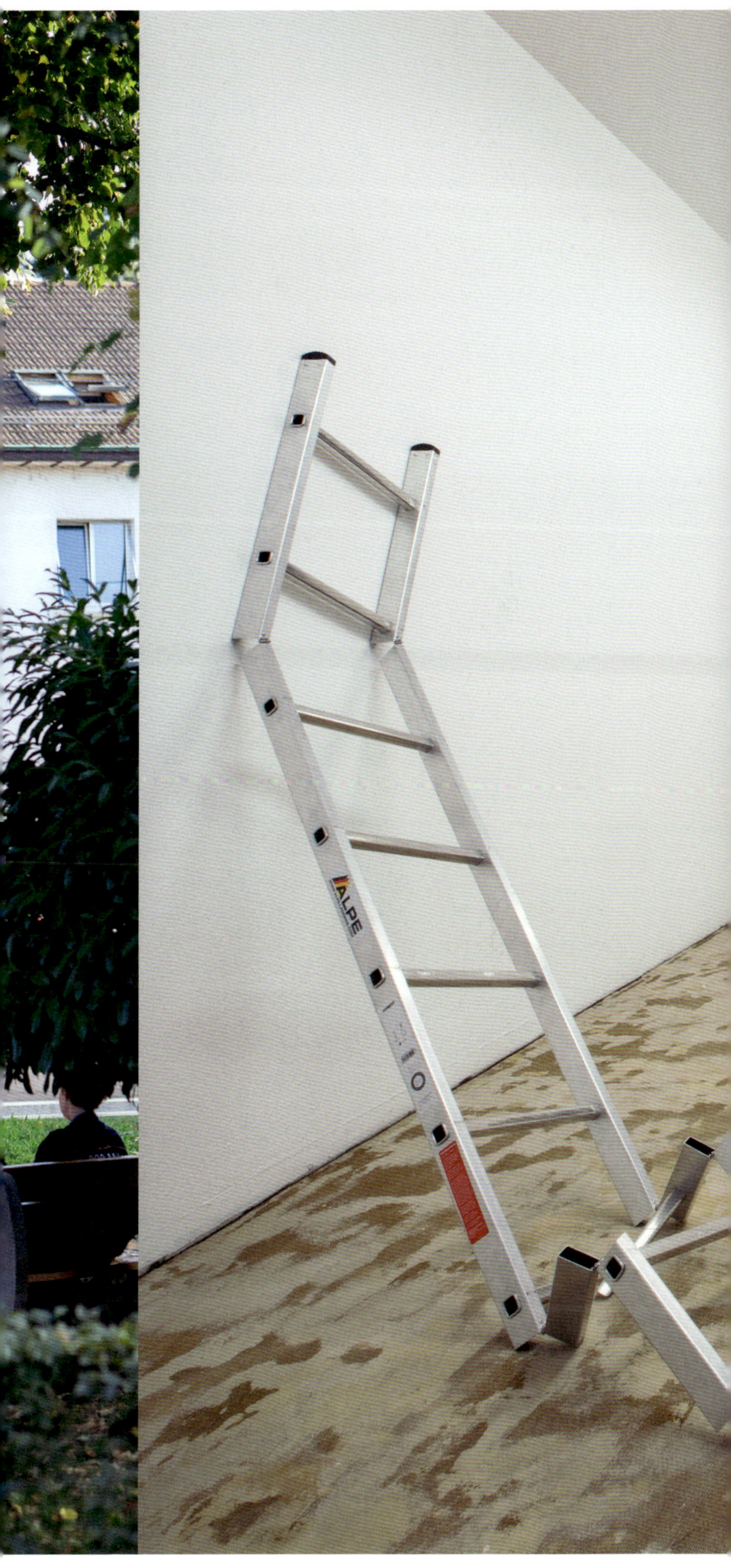

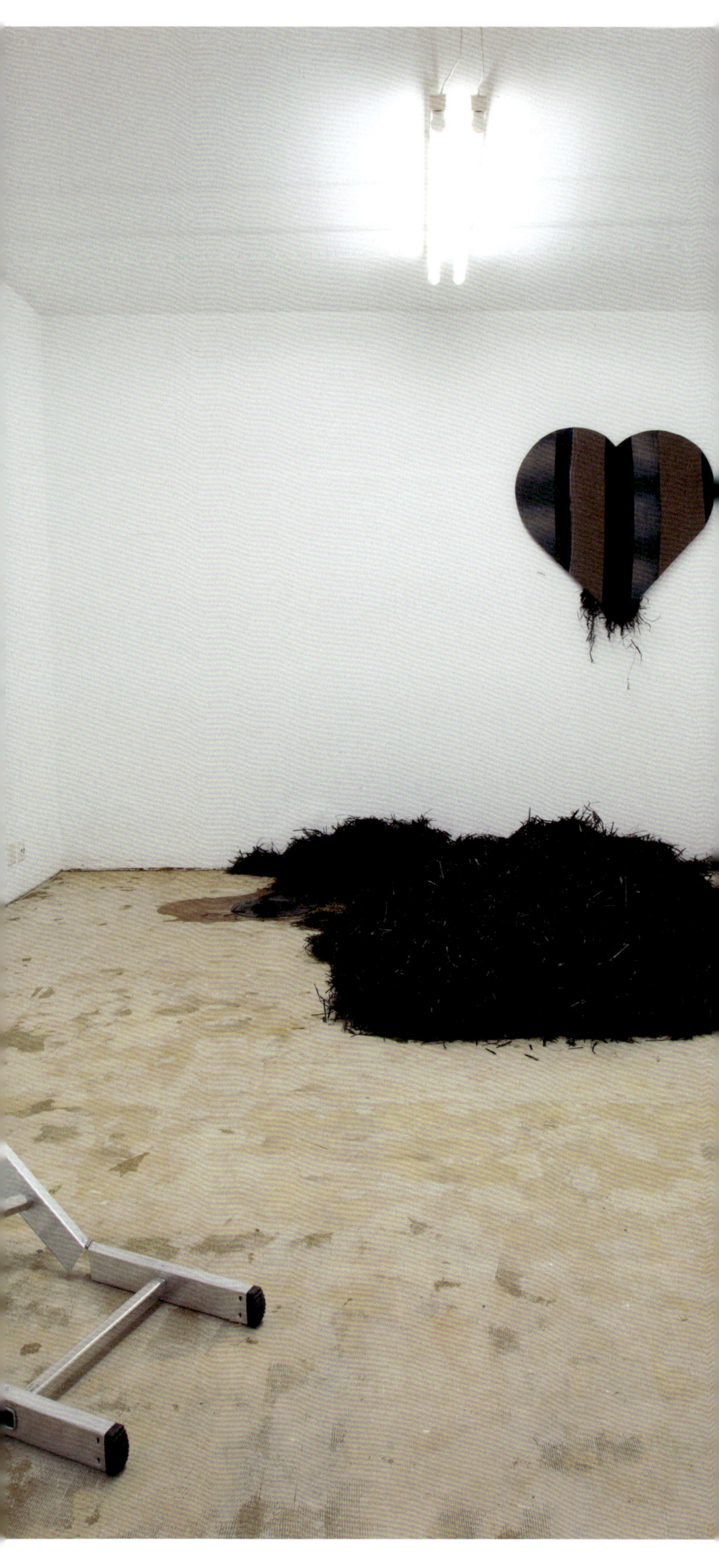

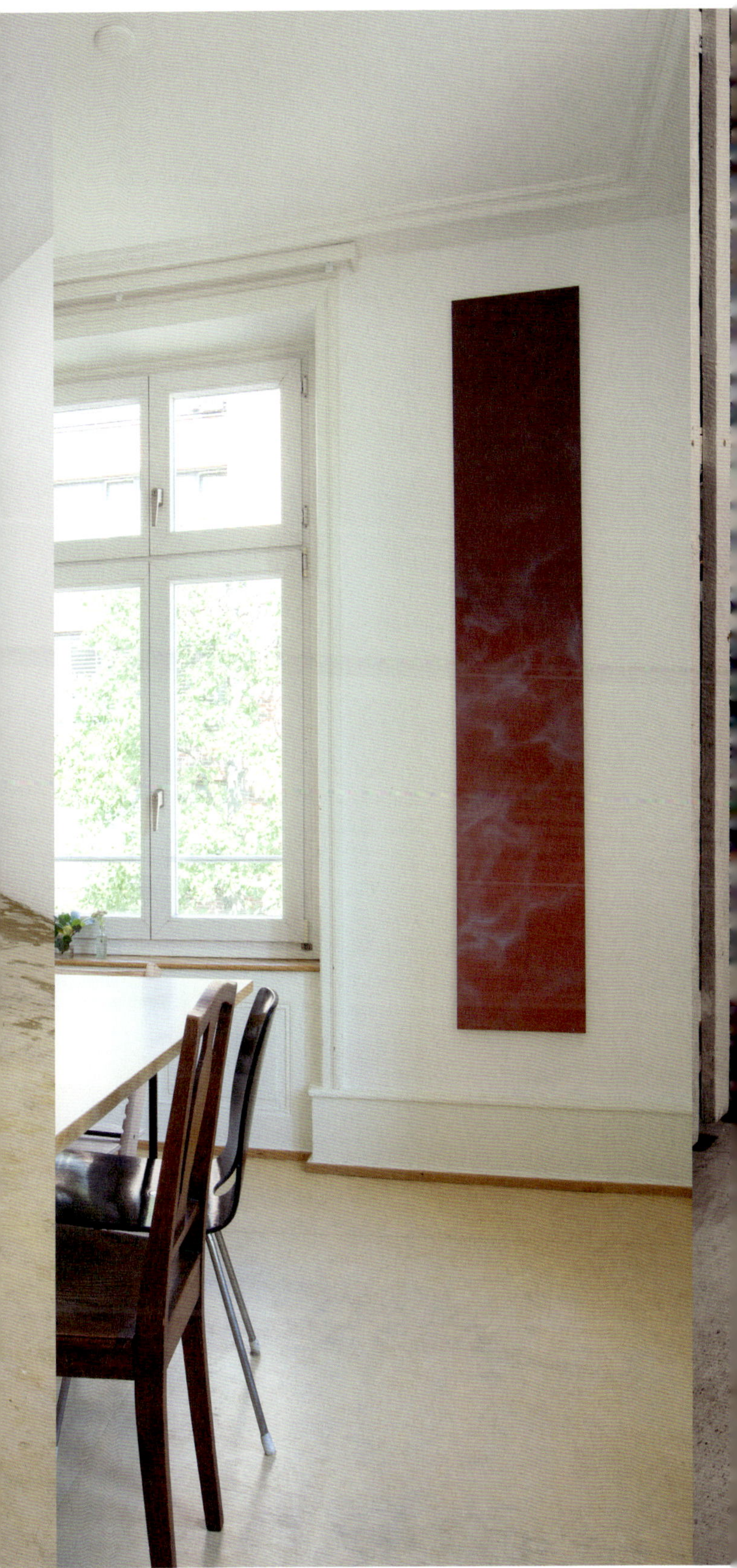

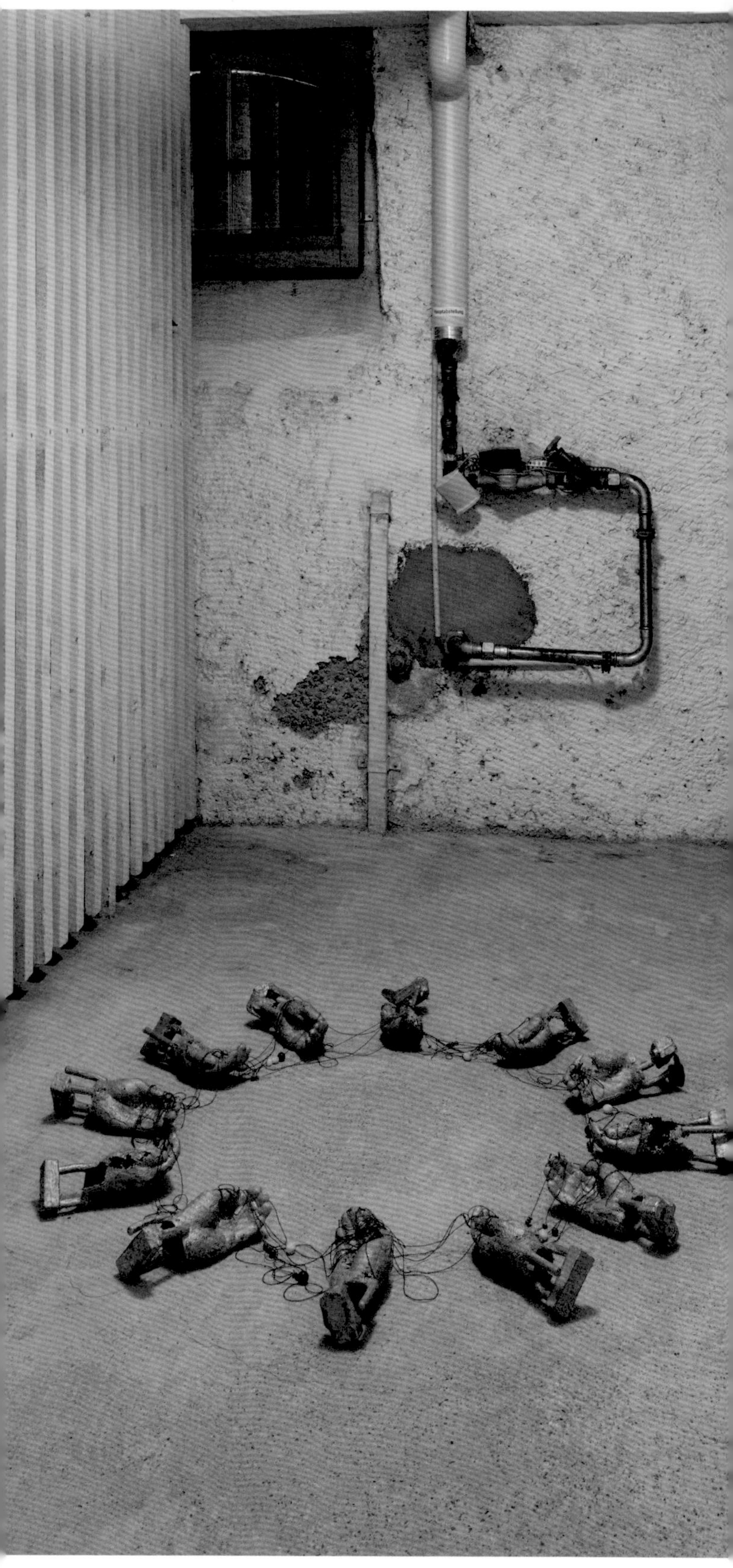

ROSA

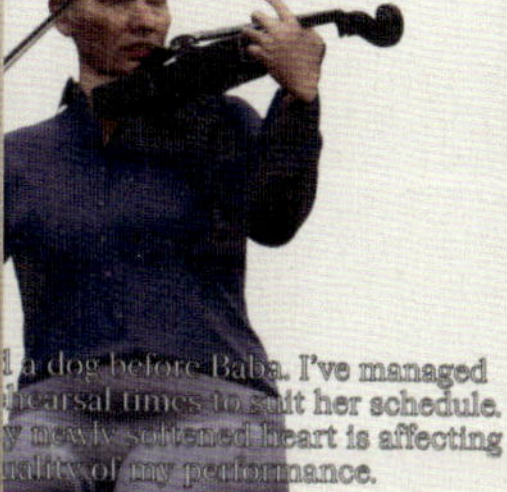

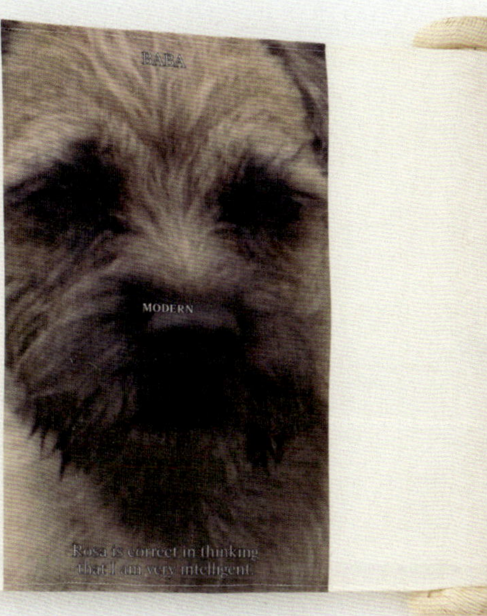

ANTONINUS PIUS CESAR   LATRINE CLEANER

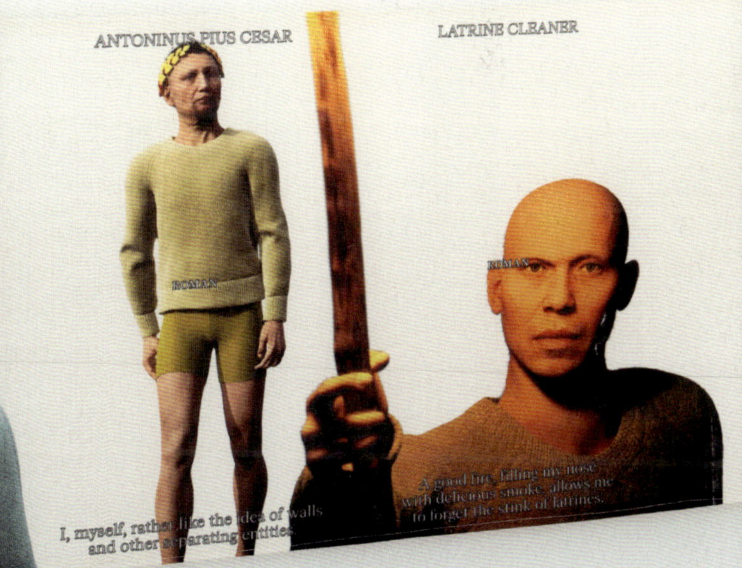

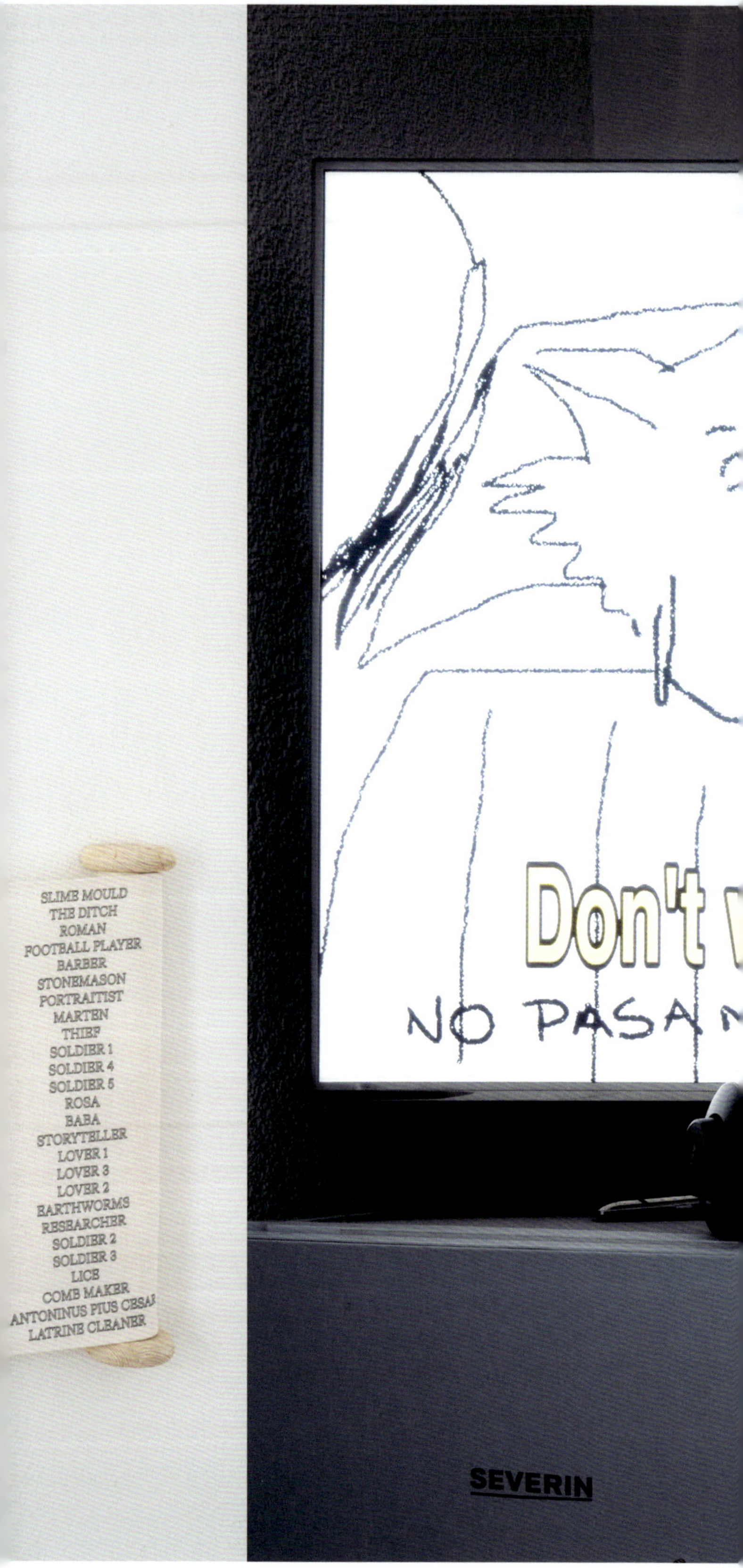

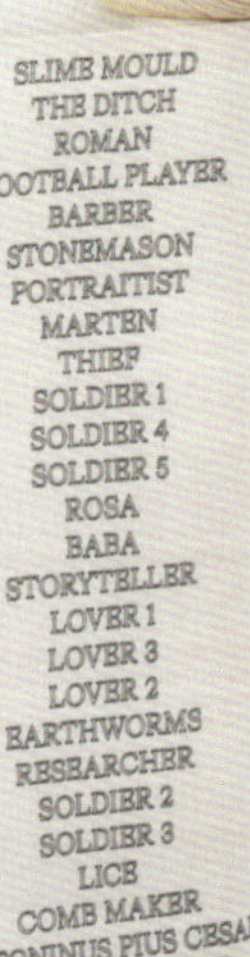

SLIME MOULD
THE DITCH
ROMAN
FOOTBALL PLAYER
BARBER
STONEMASON
PORTRAITIST
MARTEN
THIEF
SOLDIER 1
SOLDIER 4
SOLDIER 5
ROSA
BABA
STORYTELLER
LOVER 1
LOVER 3
LOVER 2
EARTHWORMS
RESEARCHER
SOLDIER 2
SOLDIER 3
LICE
COMB MAKER
ANTONINUS PIUS CESAR
LATRINE CLEANER

Don't w
NO PASAN
SEVERIN

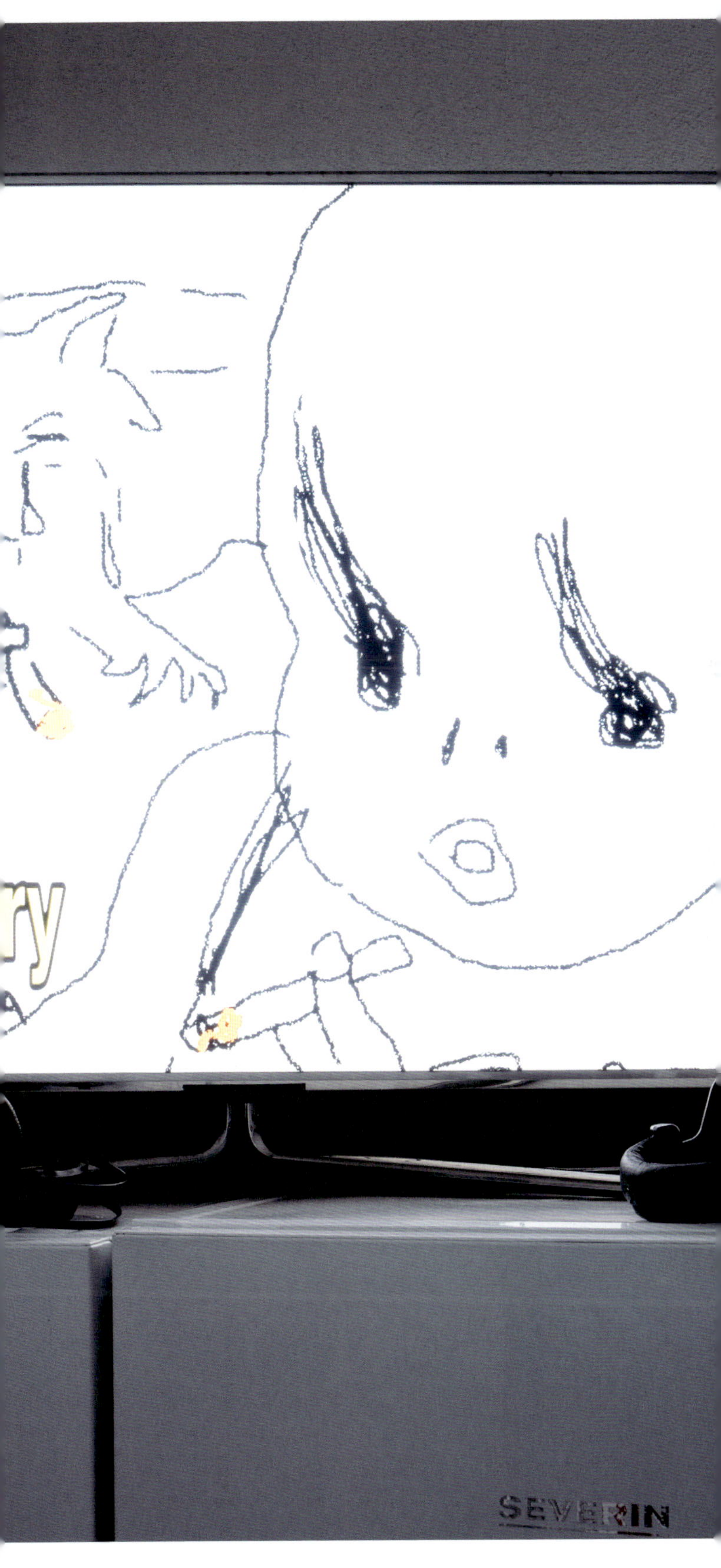

ry
SEVERIN

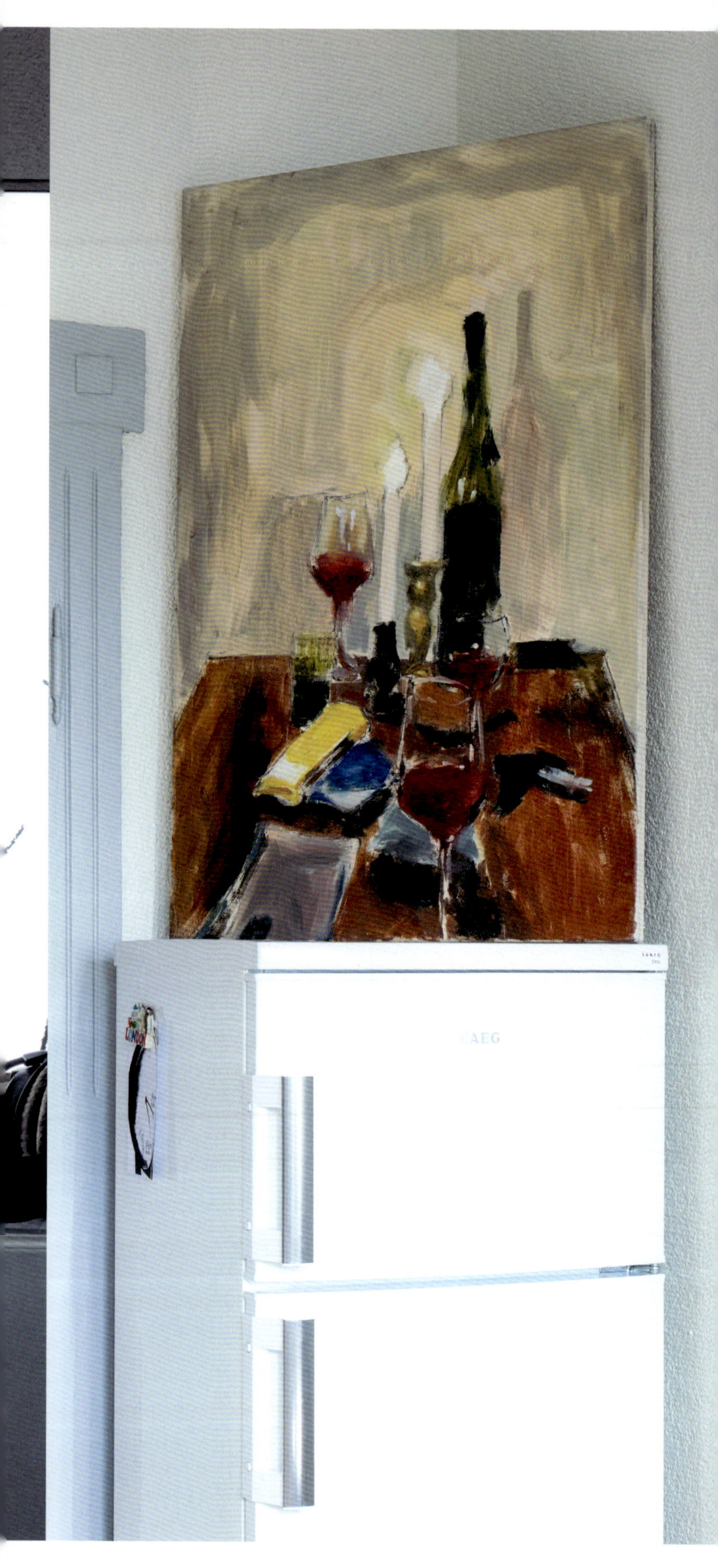

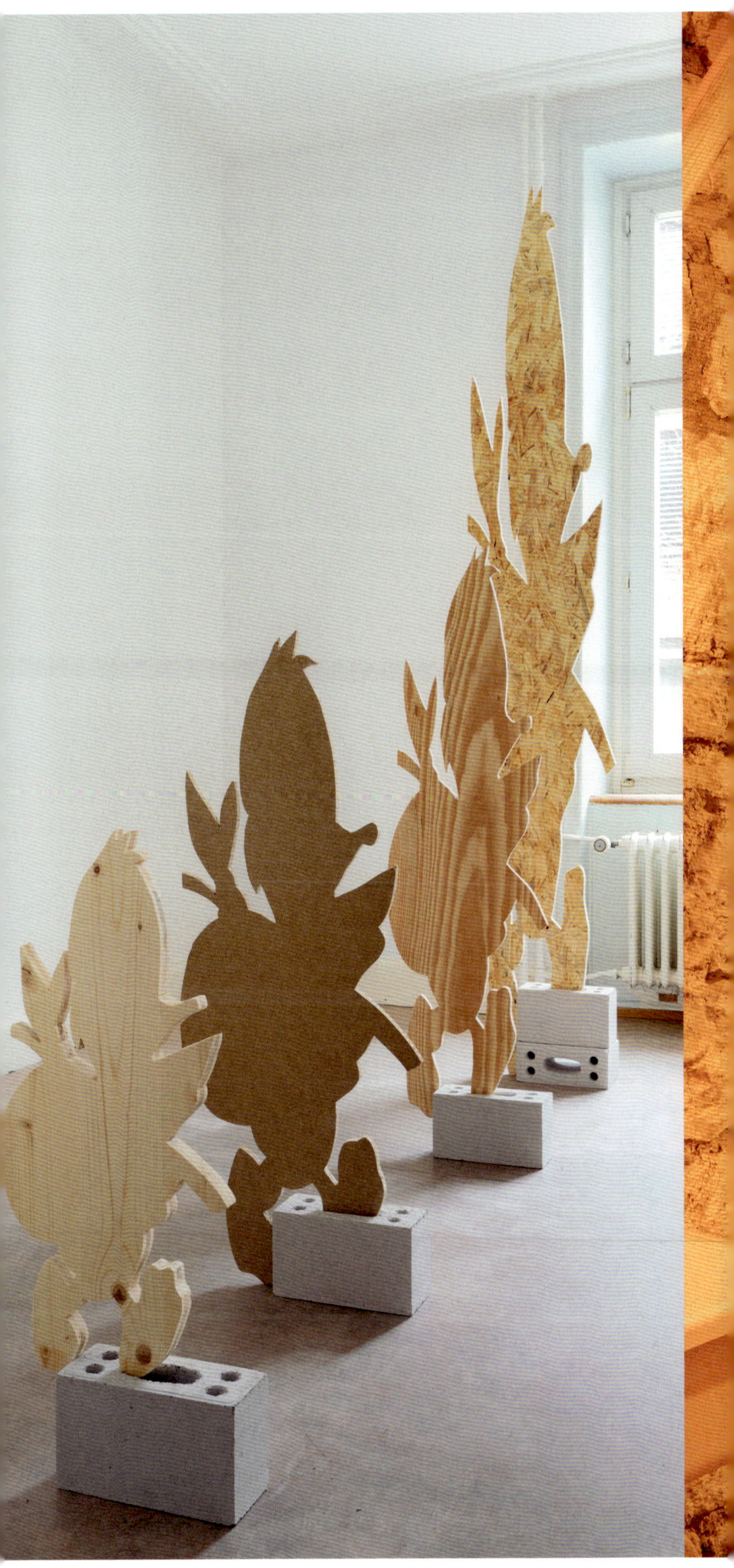

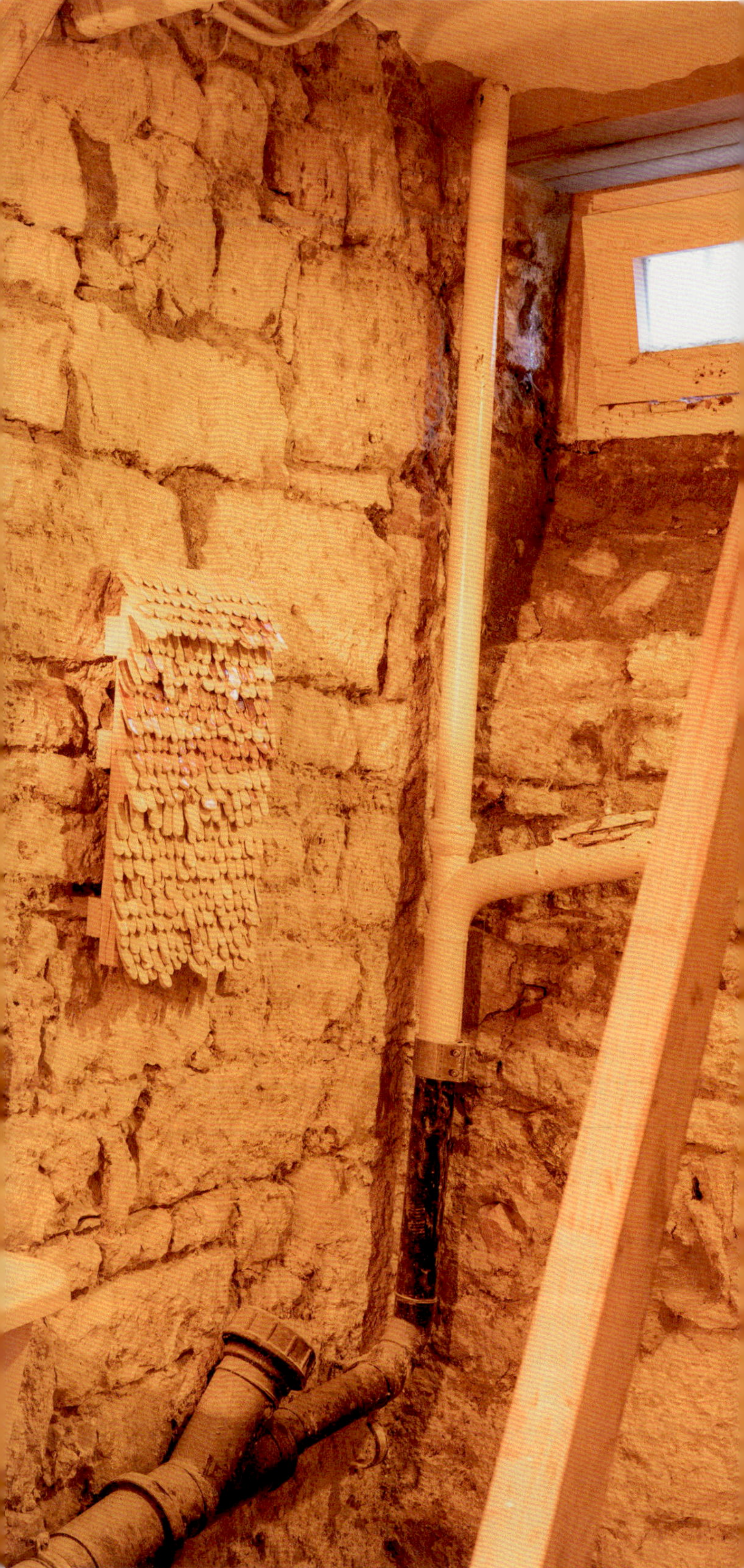

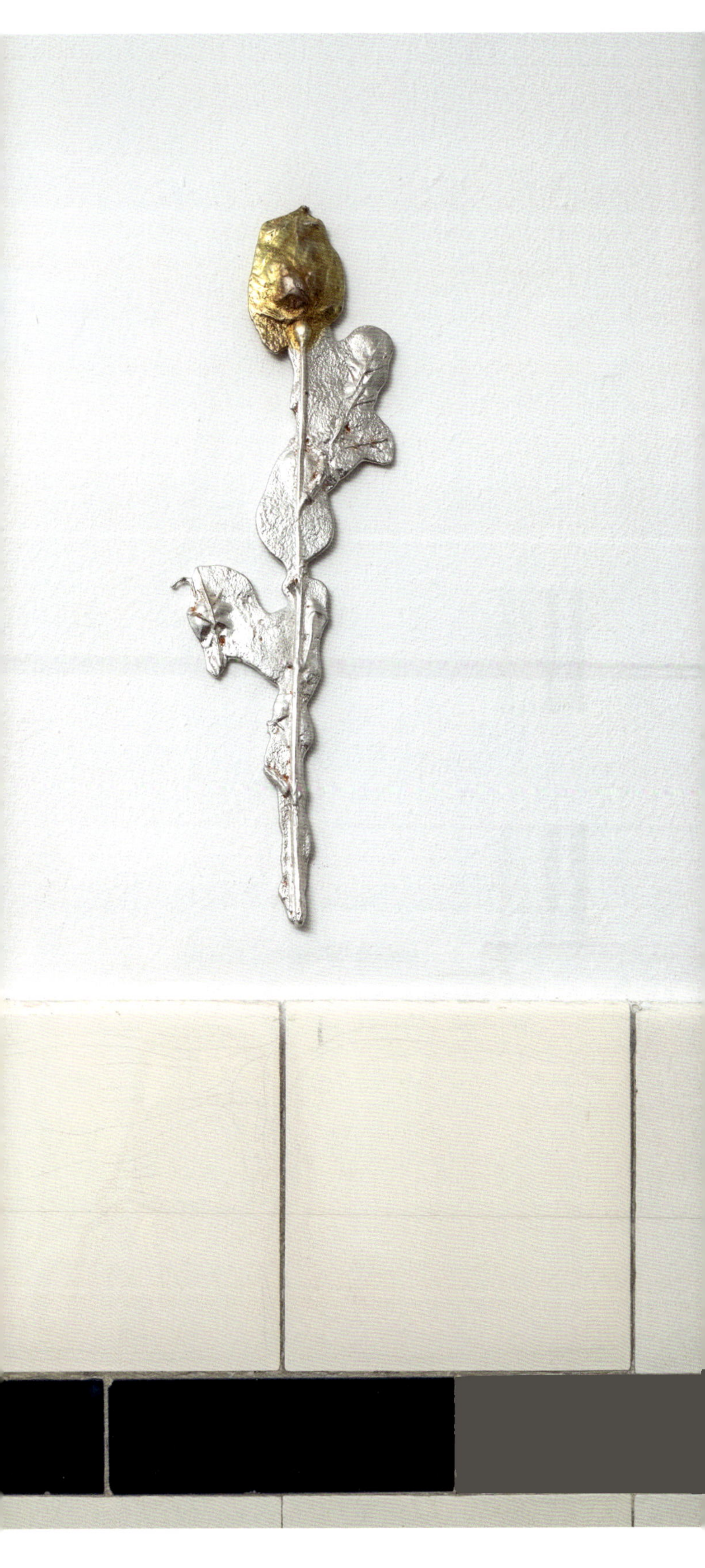

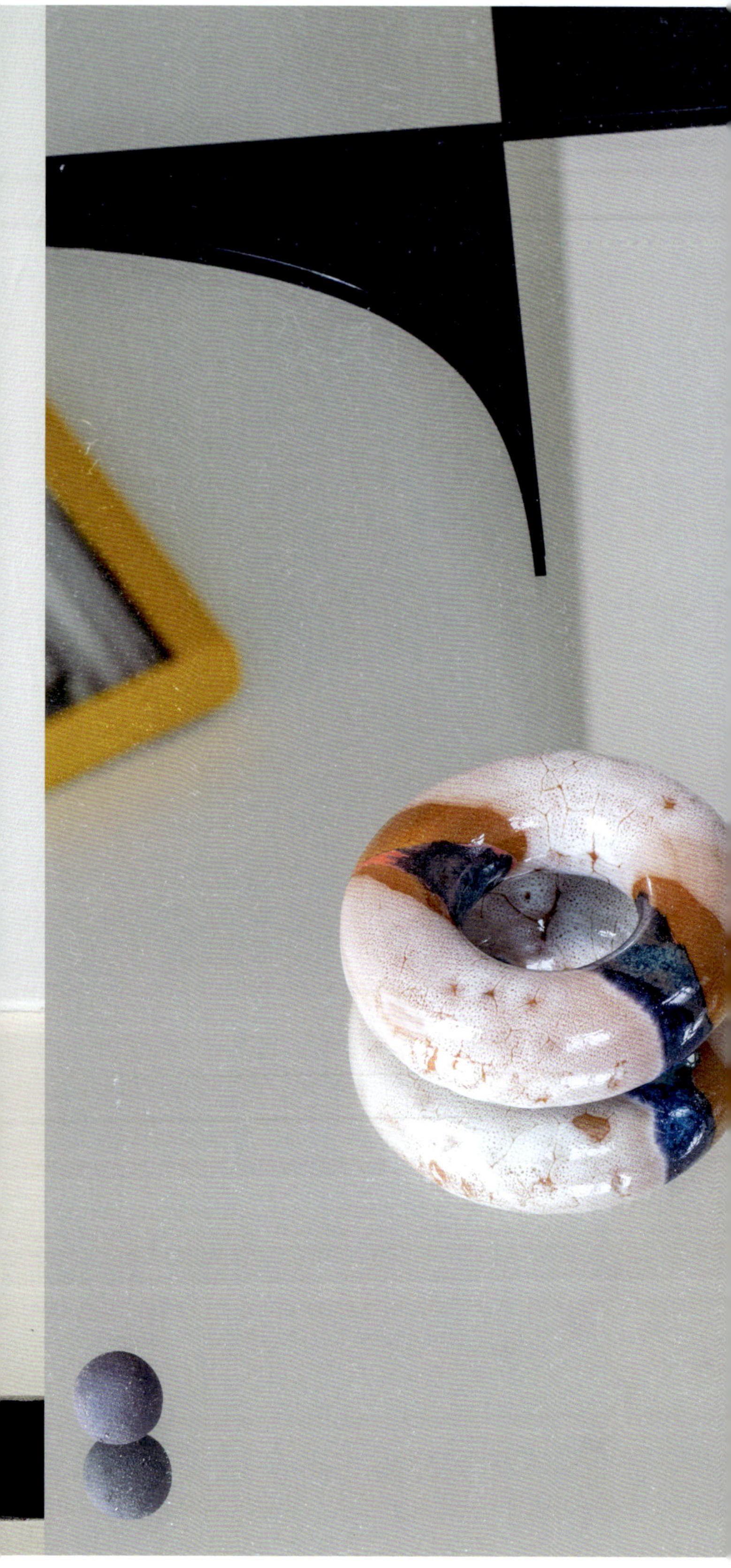

New Density

Neue Enge

Ingo Niermann

In the Western world, the average living space per person has more than doubled since the 1960s. This is accompanied by a continuous decline in the average household size. Due to an individualism that increases with education, prosperity, and social freedoms, more people live alone, couples have fewer children, and it is becoming increasingly rare for several generations of a family to live together.

Not only do smaller households inevitably require more space per person, but rising incomes and fewer children mean that people can afford more and more space. The less people live with others, the more they feel compelled and tempted to spend the bulk of their income and wealth on living space. In other words, living space replaces family—as a counterpart, as a status symbol, and as an investment to avoid being alone in old age. (Despite rising living costs, letting someone live with you is not yet frowned upon as "maintenance.") And living space does this to such an extent that even in cities where the population remains constant and new buildings are constantly being added, it is becoming so rapidly more expensive that more and more people can only afford to live there because they inherited their piece of real estate or bought it long ago.

67

Die durchschnittliche Wohnfläche pro Person hat sich in der westlichen Welt seit den 1960er Jahren mehr als verdoppelt. Dies geht mit einem kontinuierlichen Rückgang der durchschnittlichen Haushaltsgrösse einher. Aufgrund eines mit Bildung, Wohlstand und gesellschaftlichen Freiheiten zunehmenden Individualismus leben mehr Menschen als Singles, haben Paare weniger Kinder und wohnen Familien nur noch selten mehrere Generationen übergreifend zusammen.

Nicht nur, dass kleinere Haushalte unweigerlich mehr Raum pro Person beanspruchen – aufgrund gestiegener Einkommen und weniger Kinder kann man sich auch immer mehr Raum leisten. Je weniger Menschen mit anderen zusammenleben, desto mehr sehen sie sich gedrängt und verführt, den Grossteil ihres Einkommens und Vermögens für Wohnraum auszugeben. Mit anderen Worten: Wohnraum ersetzt Familie – als Gegenüber, als Statussymbol und als Investition, um im Alter nicht allein sein zu müssen. (Trotz steigender Wohnkosten ist, jemanden bei sich wohnen zu lassen, noch nicht als „Aushalten" verpönt.) Und er tut das in einem Masse, dass er sich selbst in Städten, deren Bevölkerungszahl konstant bleibt und in denen beständig hinzugebaut wird, so rasant verteuert, dass immer mehr Menschen dort nur noch zu leben vermögen, weil sie ihren geerbt oder schon vor längerer Zeit erworben haben.

Meanwhile, young people in particular, who neither earn much nor have inherited, are increasingly willing to live with their parents, grandparents, and siblings for longer, to form a residential community, or to live and work in the same place. The latter does not have to be a home office, but can also mean living in a showroom or a workshop—or, as in the case of Palazzina, all in one.

The desire for such a re-collectivization, and the reversal of the separation of living and working that occurred in the course of industrialization, is not only due to the increased cost of living, but also to the increase in loneliness. You can be just as much in love with a living space as with another person, you can be just as proud of it as of your own children, and it can also become in need of care. Thanks to AI, you can now even have constant conversations with it. But you still can't feel and smell it like a person. Many people get pets for haptic and olfactory interaction. But you can only have very limited conversations with them. Furthermore, such a relationship is one-sidedly dependent (the pets are owned by the humans), which humans have increasingly learned to condemn in the course of individualization.

68

Derweil wächst insbesondere bei jungen Menschen, die weder viel verdienen noch geerbt haben, die Bereitschaft, länger mit Eltern, Grosseltern und Geschwistern zusammenzuleben, eine Wohngemeinschaft zu bilden oder am selben Ort zu leben und zu arbeiten. Letzteres muss nicht das Homeoffice, sondern kann auch das Leben in einem Schauraum oder einer Werkstatt sein – oder wie im Fall von Palazzina alles in einem.

Der Wunsch nach einer solchen Re-Kollektivierung und Aufhebung der im Zuge der Industrialisierung erfolgten Trennung von Wohnen und Arbeiten ist nicht nur den gestiegenen Kosten für Wohnraum, sondern auch der zunehmenden Einsamkeit geschuldet. Zwar kann man in Wohnraum genauso verliebt sein wie in einen anderen Menschen, man kann auf ihn genauso stolz sein wie auf die eigenen Kinder, und er kann auch pflegebedürftig werden. Dank KI kann man sich neuerdings sogar unentwegt mit ihm unterhalten. Doch man kann ihn noch immer nicht wie einen Menschen fühlen und riechen. Viele schaffen sich für die haptische und olfaktorische Interaktion Haustiere an. Doch kann man sich mit ihnen nur sehr eingeschränkt unterhalten. Ausserdem besteht in einer solchen Beziehung ein einseitiges Abhängigkeitsverhältnis (die Tiere sind im Besitz der Menschen), das Menschen im Zuge der Individualisierung zwischen Menschen zunehmend zu ächten gelernt haben.

Once we start breaking down the spatial and temporal segmentation into clearly defined functional units (employment at the workplace, reproduction in the nuclear family, recreation on holiday, convalescence in hospital, etc.), the question arises as to why we should stop at the merging and compaction of the pre-modern era. Civilizational tribulations began with the introduction of agriculture and animal husbandry at the latest—which, in addition to environmental destruction, climate change, and enslavement, also brought about increasing isolation. Although people continued to live in extended families, these were already massively reduced in size comparison to the Stone Age hordes.

Today, the longing for the bustle of the horde lives on in nightlife. Here you can talk, dance and maybe even have sex in close proximity to others. However, such behavior is stigmatized or celebrated as an exception. People meet up late at night and consume drugs to overcome social inhibitions. Nevertheless, on the whole interaction with strangers remains limited. When dancing, people hardly touch each other. When talking, most people limit themselves to acquaintances and, at most, their acquaintances' acquaintances.

69

Beginnt man erst einmal, die räumliche und zeitliche Segmentierung in klar definierte funktionale Einheiten (Erwerbstätigkeit am Arbeitsplatz, Reproduktion in der Kleinfamilie, Erholung im Urlaub, Genesung im Krankenhaus etc.) aufzubrechen, stellt sich die Frage, weshalb man bei der Vermengung und Verdichtung der Vormoderne Halt machen soll. Das zivilisatorische Ungemach begann spätestens mit der Einführung von Ackerbau und Viehzucht – die neben Umweltzerstörung, Klimawandel und Versklavung auch bereits eine zunehmende Vereinzelung mit sich brachten. Zwar lebte man weiterhin in Grossfamilien, doch stellten diese gegenüber den steinzeitlichen Horden bereits eine massive Verkleinerung dar.

Heute lebt die Sehnsucht nach dem Getümmel der Horde im Nachtleben fort. Hier kann man dichtgedrängt reden, tanzen und vielleicht sogar Sex haben. Doch ein solches Verhalten wird als Ausnahme stigmatisiert oder zelebriert. Man trifft sich tief in der Nacht und konsumiert Drogen, um soziale Hemmungen zu überwinden. Dennoch bleibt die Interaktion mit Fremden in der Regel begrenzt. Beim Tanzen berührt man sich kaum. Beim Reden beschränken sich die meisten auf Bekannte und allenfalls noch deren Bekannte.

Je älter die Menschen werden und je mehr sich ihre Freundschaften und Liebesbeziehungen festigen, desto mehr verlieren sie das Interesse am Nachtleben, fühlen sich

As people get older and their friendships and love relationships become more solid, they lose interest in nightlife, perhaps also feel out of place, and don't consider it worth the
subsequent hangover, comedown or tinnitus. Since hookups
and dates can be arranged discreetly and in a controlled manner online, going out has also lost its appeal for those who are
"looking."

It is therefore time to think about new options for a voluntary bustle, which take place at different times of the day and
welcome everyone, provided they follow the concise house
rules. No special architecture is required for this. A room
that has been cleared out, measuring 3 by 3 by 3 meters, or
27 cubic meters or 27,000 liters, can accommodate around
300 people in terms of volume. If you fill only one-third of the
room with people and leave the remaining two-thirds free for
escape routes, anatomically unavoidable gaps, the supply of
fresh air and water, and the removal of excess heat, it can still
hold 100 people—plenty for a little bustle.

Even at rest, a person emits an average of 100 watts of
heat per hour. For 100 people it adds up to around 10 kilowatts
per hour, which can double during moderate physical activity.

70

vielleicht auch deplatziert, und finden es den folgenden
Hangover, Comedown oder Tinnitus nicht wert. Seit Hook-ups
und Dates diskret und kontrolliert online arrangiert werden
können, hat das Ausgehen auch für diejenigen, die „auf
der Suche" sind, an Attraktivität verloren.

Deshalb ist es Zeit, über neue Angebote des freiwilligen
Getümmels nachzudenken, die zu ganz unterschiedlichen
Tageszeiten stattfinden und alle willkommen heissen,
sofern sie die bündige Hausordnung einhalten. Hierfür ist
keine besondere Architektur vonnöten. Schon in ein leer-
geräumtes Zimmer von drei mal drei mal drei Metern, also
27 Kubikmetern oder 27 000 Litern, passen vom Volumen
her etwa dreihundert Menschen. Füllt man den Raum nur
zu einem Drittel mit Menschen und lässt die restlichen zwei
Drittel frei für Fluchtwege, anatomisch unvermeidliche
Zwischenräume, die Versorgung mit Frischluft und Wasser
sowie die Abfuhr überschüssiger Wärme, sind es immer-
hin noch einhundert – für ein kleines Getümmel völlig ausreichend.

Schon im Ruhezustand gibt ein Mensch pro Stunde
durchschnittlich an die 100 Watt Wärme ab. Bei hundert
Menschen ergibt sich eine Wärmeleistung von rund
10 Kilowatt pro Stunde, die sich mit mässiger körperlicher
Betätigung noch verdoppeln lässt. Das ist mehr als genug,
um eine Sauna von der Grösse des besagten Raumes auf
100 Grad zu erhitzen oder eine mässig isolierte Villa von der

That is more than enough to heat a sauna the size of the room in question to 100 degrees Celsius or to comfortably heat a poorly insulated villa the size of the current Palazzina on a winter's day. The sweat produced in a bustle—at sauna temperatures, up to four liters per person per hour—makes watering house plants redundant. The collected condensation can be used for showering, washing dishes, and bathing. A domestic bustle is therefore attractive for ecological reasons alone.

But how do you manage to create a bustle repeatedly at home? Since the field of vision is severely restricted for most participants, visual presentations and screenings are only of limited use as attractors. Acoustic presentations are also problematic, since the crowdedness requires continuous communication about pressure points, desired position changes or escape routes.

It is more advantageous to focus on the bustle itself and to try out practices that reduce the risk of tussles and assaults, that allow physical proximity to strangers to be experienced as consistently euphoric, and that raise awareness of the specific needs or fears of the people around you. This ensures that the bustle is not, as is often the case in nightlife, defined

71

Grösse des heutigen Palazzinas an einem Wintertag wohlig zu beheizen. Die Schweissproduktion eines Getümmels – bei Saunatemperaturen bis zu vier Liter pro Mensch und Stunde – macht das Bewässern von Zimmerpflanzen überflüssig. Aufgefangenes Kondenswasser kann zum Duschen, Spülen und Waschen genutzt werden. Ein häusliches Getümmel ist also allein schon aus ökologischen Gründen attraktiv.

Wie aber schafft man es, bei sich daheim wiederholt ein Getümmel zu kreieren? Da das Sichtfeld hierbei für die meisten stark eingeschränkt ist, kommen visuelle Präsentationen und Screenings als Attraktoren nur bedingt in Frage. Akustische Präsentationen sind ebenfalls problematisch, da die grosse Enge eine fortlaufende Kommunikation über Druckstellen, gewünschte Positionswechsel oder Auswege erfordert.

Vorteilhafter ist es, das Getümmel als solches in den Fokus zu rücken und Praktiken zu erproben, die die Gefahr von Rangeleien und Übergriffen reduzieren, die körperliche Nähe zu Fremden als durchweg euphorisierend erfahrbar machen und für konkrete Bedürfnisse oder Ängste der umgebenden Menschen sensibilisieren. So trägt man Sorge, dass das Getümmel nicht, wie im Nachtleben oft der Fall, von Konkurrenz und unerfülltem Verlangen bestimmt ist, sondern von umfassender Fürsorge und Liebe.

Neulinge und von besonderen körperlichen oder sozialen Aversionen Betroffene sind eingeladen, sich bereits eine

by competition and unfulfilled desire, but by all-encompassing
care and love.

Newcomers and those affected by particular physical or
social aversions are invited to meet an hour before the actual
bustle to practice getting close to each other without touch-
ing. To do this, you form small groups in which you explore
each other's presumed aura or, in a manner similar to the
game Tetris, attempt to reform yourselves repeatedly, keeping the spaces between you as small as possible. Both can
initially be tried out with objects.

In the next phase, groups of up to twenty people are
formed, within which you touch as many others as possible
at the same time. Initially, you try to find a comfortable resting
position for everyone without using words. You remain in this
position until it becomes uncomfortable for the first person.
Then the search for a comfortable resting position for everyone begins again. After repeating this exercise for a quarter of
an hour, the groups begin to move slowly through the room in a
compact contact improvisation and merge with other groups.
In doing so, you ensure that everyone has an outside and can
withdraw at any time without further ado.

72

Stunde vor dem eigentlichen Getümmel zu treffen, um sich
zunächst in grosser Nähe zu üben, ohne sich zu berühren.
Hierfür bilden sie kleine Gruppen, in denen sie gegenseitig
ihre mutmassliche Aura abfahren oder ähnlich wie beim
Spiel Tetris versuchen, sich immer wieder neu kompakt zu
formieren und dabei die Zwischenräume untereinander
so klein wie möglich zu gestalten. Beides kann zunächst auch
mit Objekten erprobt werden.

In einer nächsten Phase werden Gruppen von bis zu
zwanzig Personen gebildet, innerhalb derer man sich
mit möglichst vielen gleichzeitig berührt. Hierbei versucht
man zunächst, ohne Worte eine für alle angenehme
Ruheposition zu finden. In dieser verharrt man so lange,
bis sie der ersten Person unbequem wird. Daraufhin beginnt
die Suche nach einer für alle angenehmen Ruheposition
von neuem. Nachdem man diese Übung eine Viertelstunde
lang wiederholt hat, beginnen die Gruppen, sich in einer
kompakten Kontaktimprovisation langsam durch den Raum
zu bewegen und mit anderen Gruppen zu verschmelzen.
Hierbei bleibt man darauf bedacht, dass alle ein Aussen
haben und sich jederzeit ohne weiteres entziehen können.

Im eigentlichen Getümmel bilden die physisch und
psychisch Robustesten den liegenden Bodensatz, über den
sich der Rest der Anwesenden vorsichtig ergiesst. Alter-
nativ stellen sich die Anwesenden dicht gedrängt in den
Raum, um sich dann gemeinsam langsam und vorsichtig in

In the actual bustle, the physically and mentally most robust lie down and form the base, over which the rest of you carefully pour. Alternatively, you stand close together in the room and then slowly and carefully push each other in different directions—a mosh pit in slow motion. On top, you carry a layer of people—more stage-topping than diving. As soon as someone signals "Stop!" you relieve that person, give them air and the opportunity to quickly leave the room. After an hour at the latest, the bustle ends to avoid exhaustion, which is all too great and ignored in euphoria.

INGO NIERMANN is a writer and an artist. Recently published projects include the book *The Monadic Age: Notes on the Coming Social Order* (2024), the video diptych *Walder/Eigner* (2023/24, with Erik Niedling), the podcast series *Ocean Wants* (2021), and the video series *Deutsch Süd-Ost* (2020). Niermann is a lecturer at the Institute Art Gender Nature, HGK Basel FNHW.

verschiedene Richtungen zu schieben – Moshing in Zeitlupe. Obenauf trägt man eine liegende Schicht von Menschen – mehr Stagetopping als -diving. Sobald jemand „Stop!" signalisiert, entlastet man diese Person, gibt ihr Luft und die Gelegenheit, den Raum zügig zu verlassen. Nach spätestens einer Stunde endet das Getümmel, um eine allzu grosse, in der Euphorie ausgeblendete Erschöpfung zu vermeiden.

INGO NIERMANN ist Schriftsteller und Künstler. Zu seinen zuletzt veröffentlichten Projekten gehören das Buch *The Monadic Age: Notes on the Coming Social Order* (2024), das Video-Diptychon *Walder/Eigner* (2023/2024, mit Erik Niedling), die Podcast-Serie *Ocean Wants* (2021) und die Video-Serie *Deutsch Süd-Ost* (2020). Niermann ist Dozent am Institut Kunst Gender Natur, HGK Basel FNHW.

Five Years of Artistic Hospitality

Fünf Jahre künstlerische Gastgeschenke

Ines Goldbach

It all starts with friendship. A friendship that expands into incredible hospitality and at the same time seeks out the unknown in order to understand it and, above all, integrate it. This is not only something unique, something extraordinary, the powerful driving force, the beginning that triggers and motivates everything, but—to put it simply—the heartbeat that everything depends upon. So, the first question is already clear: in the years to come, will it be possible to continue to weave this delicate yet vital bond of friendship, trust, and unbounded hospitality and, most importantly, to pass it on to people other than the founders?

When we meet for this conversation, there have been numerous meetings, visits, exhibitions, houses, days, and seasons over the past five years of Palazzina. One thing remains constant: the current third location on Baslerstrasse in Allschwil, where the Palazzina collective is currently based, continues to be hive of activity. In the courtyards, bicycles are leaning against walls and garden fences; doors and gates are left open. The doorbell label is also very telling: "Palazzina. Ring Everywhere." There is always someone to energetically welcome you in.

75

Am Anfang steht die Freundschaft. Eine Freundschaft, die sich zu einer unglaublichen Gastfreundschaft ausweitet und zugleich das Unbekannte sucht, um es zu erfassen und vor allem zu integrieren. Dies ist nicht nur das Unikate, das Aussergewöhnliche, der gewaltige Motor, der Beginn, der alles mit sich zieht und bewegt, sondern – um es vorwegzunehmen – der Herzschlag, mit dem alles steht und fällt. Damit steht die Eingangsfrage bereits fest: Wird es in den kommenden Jahren gelingen, dieses feine und zugleich existenzielle Band aus Freundschaft, Vertrauen und grenzenloser Gastgeber*innenschaft weiterzuflechten und vor allem an andere Menschen als die Gründer*innen weiterzugeben?

Viele Treffen, Besuche, Ausstellungen, Häuser, Tages- und Jahreszeiten in den vergangenen fünf Jahren liegen hinter dem Palazzina, als wir uns für das aktuelle Gespräch treffen. Eines bleibt konstant: Auch am gegenwärtigen dritten Standort in Allschwil an der Baslerstrasse, wo das Kollektiv Palazzina aktuell seinen Sitz hat, herrscht reges Treiben. Velos stehen im Innenhof, an Hauswände oder Gartenzäune gelehnt, Haus- und Gartentüren sind geöffnet. Sehr bezeichnend ist auch die Beschriftung der Klingelbox: „Palazzina. Überall klingeln." Und so gibt es immer jemanden, die*er tatkräftig zum Einlass empfängt.

The kitchens—there are currently three—are busy. Someone is usually cooking, chopping, or tidying somewhere. The Bialetti coffee machine on the stove is full at all times and there is always something on offer for new arrivals. People sit down together at the table, exchange ideas and, of course, are surrounded by what Palazzina is all about: people and works of art by artists from all over Switzerland, who are often, but not always, already on friendly terms with the collective that invited them there and belong to the same generation as the initiators themselves. Friendships in all their forms are both nurtured and developed here.

It's easy to tell the story of how they found each other, because one thing led to another like a string of pearls: the artist Claudia Müller, who was teaching in Geneva, drew the attention of her friend, the artist Noemi Pfister—who had already been living in the Bachletten neighborhood of Basel for a year at that point—to a house on Schweizergasse that was available for interim use and perfectly suited for a low-cost shared apartment. Together with another artist friend, Victoria Holdt, this was exactly what they wanted. Around the same time, the artist Simone Holliger, who was still living in Geneva, was looking for a new place to live with her partner

Die Küchen – aktuell drei an der Zahl – sind belebt. Meist wird irgendwo gekocht, geschnippelt, geräumt. Eine stets gefüllte Bialetti-Kaffeemaschine steht auf dem Herd, es gibt immer etwas, das den Ankommenden angeboten wird. Man setzt sich gemeinsam an den Tisch, tauscht sich aus und ist natürlich längst umgeben von dem, was das Palazzina ausmacht: Menschen und Kunstwerke von Kunstschaffenden aus der ganzen Schweiz, die oft, aber nicht immer von Anbeginn mit dem einladenden Kollektiv freundschaftlich verbunden sind und der gleichen Generation angehören wie die Initiierenden selbst. Hier wird Freundschaft in allen Fasern gelebt und zugleich neu aufgebaut.

Wie sie sich gefunden haben, lässt sich gut erzählen, denn wie bei einer Perlenkette kam eines zum anderen: Die befreundete Künstlerin Claudia Müller, die in Genf lehrte, machte die Künstlerin Noemi Pfister, die bereits seit einem Jahr im Bachlettenquartier in Basel wohnte, auf ein Haus in der Schweizergasse aufmerksam, das zur Zwischennutzung frei stand und sich ideal für eine kostengünstige Wohngemeinschaft eignete. Zusammen mit der befreundeten Künstlerin Victoria Holdt entsprach dies ganz ihrem gemeinsamen Wunsch. Parallel dazu suchte die Künstlerin Simone Holliger, die noch in Genf lebte, mit ihrem Partner Mathieu Dafflon und ihrer Tochter Tilda eine neue Bleibe. Bald darauf zogen noch die Künstler*innen Géraldine Honauer

Mathieu Dafflon and their daughter Tilda. Soon afterward, the artists Géraldine Honauer and Luca Rossi Dossi moved into the newly found house. When Simone Holliger and her family temporarily left for Berlin, artist Kelly Tissot and art historian Ines Tondar moved in, initially as temporary tenants—and decided to stay. They started out a little naively, explains Noemi Pfister with a laugh, as they had no real experience with exhibitions and everything that goes along with them: "We were and are all artists or people who are very closely connected to art."

And suddenly there was much more room than they needed to live in, and the structure of the ground floor—like a showcase, with large windows facing the street—brought the inside out and vice versa. Why not use this space as it was almost naturally intended? And so they invited artist friends or people whose work they wanted to immerse themselves in, and presented their work on the ground floor, while they lived on the other three floors, with two rooms each.

I can remember my first encounter with this offspace well, which was initially mainly run by women. Driving around this purely residential area, which was dominated by buildings from the turn of the century and from the 1970s and 1980s,

und Luca Rossi Dossi in das neu gefundene Haus. Als Simone Holliger mit der Familie vorübergehend nach Berlin aufbrach, rückten zunächst zur Zwischenmiete die Künstlerin Kelly Tissot und die Kunsthistorikerin Ines Tondar nach – und beschlossen zu bleiben. Man habe etwas naiv begonnen, erzählt Noemi Pfister lachend im Gespräch, da man ja noch keine rechte Erfahrung gehabt habe mit Ausstellungen und allem, was dazugehört: „Wir waren und sind alle Künstler*innen oder Personen, die der Kunst sehr nahe stehen."

Und plötzlich gab es da viel mehr Platz als man zum Wohnen brauchte, und eine Raumstruktur im Erdgeschoss, die – vitrinenartig und mit grossen Fenstern zur Strasse hin – das Innen nach aussen holte und umgekehrt. Warum also diesen Raum nicht nutzen, quasi als natürliche Konsequenz? Und so lud man befreundete Kunstschaffende ein oder solche, in deren Werk man selbst gerne eintauchen wollte, und präsentierte deren Arbeiten im Erdgeschoss, während man in den anderen drei Etagen, jede mit zwei Zimmern, wohnte.

Ich erinnere mich gut an meine erste Begegnung mit diesem Offspace, der anfangs mehrheitlich von Frauen getragen wurde. Man fuhr um die Ecken des reinen Wohnviertels, das von Gebäuden aus der Jahrhundertwende und Bauten der 1970er bis 1980er Jahre geprägt war. Plötzlich tauchte an einem eher unscheinbaren Mehrfamilienhaus

you suddenly came across the word Palazzina in large letters on a rather inconspicuous apartment building from the 1970s that was about to be demolished. Almost like a promise and a belief in beauty and grandeur—that's what the name suggested to me: an Italian beauty, without exaggeration, a simple beauty that this place could achieve through art.

And so it came to pass: the program ran for the entire year of the interim use period, from November 2019 to June 2020, with seven exhibitions by sixteen artists. The initiators invited other artists living in Switzerland; different people took the lead for each of the exhibitions, while others took care of the budget, external funding, communications, or even the vernissage and catering. The challenges of the pandemic were also managed together, aided by the exhibition architecture that resembled a display case and also allowed people to look in from the outside.

After this year of interim use in the Bachletten neighborhood, a renewed search for the next opportunity and more space began. The original six people had now grown to eight, who all wanted to continue the project if a suitable location could be found. According to Ines Tondar, this was a moment when anything could have happened: the group could have

aus den 1970er Jahren, das kurz vor dem Abriss stand, in grossen Lettern das Wort Palazzina auf. Fast wie ein Versprechen und der Glaube an eine Schönheit und Grösse – das suggerierte mir der Name: eine italienische Schönheit, nicht übertrieben, eine schlichte Schönheit, die dieser Ort eben durch die Kunst werden könnte.

Und so kam es denn auch: Das Programm lief während des gesamten Jahres der Zwischennutzung, von November 2019 bis Juni 2020, mit sieben Ausstellungen von sechzehn Kunstschaffenden. Die Initiierenden luden weitere in der Schweiz lebende Kunstschaffende ein; mal war die*er eine, mal die*er andere stärker für die Ausstellung verantwortlich, während sich andere um Budget, Drittmittel, Kommunikation oder auch die Vernissage und Catering kümmerten. Auch die Herausforderungen der Pandemie wurden gemeinsam gestemmt, begünstigt durch die vitrinenartige Ausstellungsarchitektur, die Einblicke auch von aussen gewährte.

Nach dieser rund einjährigen Zwischennutzung im Bachlettenquartier begann eine erneute Suche nach einer neuen Möglichkeit sowie nach mehr Raum. Aus den ursprünglich sechs Personen waren mittlerweile acht geworden, die das Projekt weiterführen wollten, sofern sich ein geeigneter Ort finden liesse. Das sei ein Moment gewesen, so Ines Tondar, in dem alles hätte passieren können: Die Gruppe

split up and gone their separate ways, or they could have worked together to find a place that would constitute the next step.

The new house in Alemannengasse—a former children's psychiatric hospital—proved to be ideal. With four floors, fourteen rooms, a kitchen, and four bathrooms, the young family had their own private space, as did all the other members of the collective. Artists Katrin Niedermeier, Joan Pallé, Joaquim Cantor Miranda, Nicolás Sarmiento, and Ester Alemayehu Hatle joined the group—some stayed for longer periods, others only as temporary tenants. The exhibition space was also expanded to include additional rooms in the building.

It's always amazing how everything comes together to form a whole, says Simone Holliger, who has just returned from a year in Rome with her partner and their daughter Tilda. After all, everyone has a thousand things of their own to get on with: their own work, their own projects, their private lives, family lives, and so on. Nevertheless, their joint commitment to the Palazzina project is always at the forefront. The invitations to the artists, Holliger continues, heavily depend on the artistic interest in each other's work—on how both the hosts and the invited guests understand themselves as artists. Furthermore,

hätte auseinanderbrechen und getrennte Wege einschlagen können – stattdessen wurde gemeinschaftlich ein Ort gefunden, der einen weiteren Schritt darstellte.

Das neue Haus in der Alemannengasse – eine ehemalige Kinderpsychiatrie – erwies sich als ideal. Mit vier Stockwerken, vierzehn Zimmern, einer Küche und vier Bädern hatte sowohl die junge Familie ihren privaten Raum als auch alle anderen Mitglieder des Kollektivs. So kamen die Kunstschaffenden Katrin Niedermeier, Joan Pallé, Joaquim Cantor Miranda, Nicolás Sarmiento und Ester Alemayehu Hatle dazu – die einen blieben länger, andere nur zu kurzen Zwischenmieten. Zudem konnte die sogenannte Ausstellungsfläche um zusätzliche Räume im Haus erweitert werden.

Es sei doch immer wieder erstaunlich, wie sich alles zu einem Ganzen zusammenfüge, so Simone Holliger, die gerade mit ihrem Partner und der gemeinsamen Tochter Tilda von einem Jahr in Rom zurückgekehrt ist. Denn jeder habe ja seine eigenen tausend Dinge voranzutreiben: das eigene Werk, die eigenen Projekte, das Private, Familiäre und so weiter. Dennoch stehe das gemeinschaftliche Engagement für das Projekt Palazzina immer wieder im Vordergrund. Die Einladung an die Kunstschaffenden, so Holliger weiter, hänge stark vom künstlerischen Interesse an deren jeweiliger Arbeit ab – sowohl vom künstlerischen Selbstverständnis, das man selbst verfolge, als auch von

as Nicolás Sarmiento once put it, much more can be achieved as a group than on one's own. This is also clear from the many discussions, openings, and encounters—the focus is not on the individual, but on the power of the community.

And how do you find new housemates, I ask the group, especially when it's about much more than just living together? In addition to the human aspect, the main question is whether people want to participate in the Palazzina project, explains Noemi Pfister. And so far, there hasn't been anyone who hasn't joined in, apart from those who have only been there temporarily for an interim period or subletting, usually only for a few weeks. And of course, not everyone wants to live like this, Holliger adds with a laugh. That is probably what makes this whole set-up so special. What's more, this mutual artistic understanding grows as a result of not only sharing interests and getting to know fellow colleagues, but also doing a lot of things together, whether visiting exhibitions and other projects or simply going out for a beer together.

But something else becomes clear in the course of this conversation: the most exciting moments are the days just before a vernissage, when everything is condensed into one

jenem, das die Eingeladenen verfolgen würden. Ausserdem, so formulierte es Nicolás Sarmiento einmal, lasse sich als Gruppe viel mehr umsetzen als im Alleingang. Das wird auch anhand der vielen Gespräche, Eröffnungen und Begegnungen deutlich – nicht die*er Einzelne steht im Vordergrund, sondern die Kraft der Gemeinschaft.

Und wie findet man neue Mitbewohner*innen, frage ich die Gruppe, gerade wenn es um sehr viel mehr geht als nur ums Mitwohnen? Da stelle sich neben dem menschlichen Aspekt in erster Linie die Frage, ob man sich am Projekt Palazzina beteiligen wolle, erklärt Noemi Pfister. Und so habe es bisher noch niemanden gegeben, der nicht mitgemacht hätte, ausser jenen, die nur kurz zur Zwischennutzung oder Untermiete da waren, meist nur für wenige Wochen. Und natürlich habe nicht jede*r Lust, so zu leben, fügt Holliger lachend hinzu. Das sei wohl auch das Besondere an dieser Gesamtkonstellation. Zudem wachse das gemeinsame künstlerische Verständnis dadurch, dass man nicht nur Interessen teile und gemeinsam befreundete Kolleg*innen kennenlerne, sondern auch viel zusammen unternehme, sei es der Besuch von Ausstellungen und Projekten oder auch einfach mal gemeinsam ein Bier trinken zu gehen.

Im Gespräch wird aber noch etwas deutlich: Die spannendsten Momente sind die Tage kurz vor der Vernissage, wenn alles auf einen Punkt komprimiert wird und

place and comes together. That's when the energy is concentrated. That's when everyone tries to be present around the clock and do their bit—whether by hanging works, moving carpets and shelves out of the way, or cooking for the vernissage guests.

People may remember the 1970s and 1980s, when artists first set out to explore new horizons and, above all, the unknown worlds beyond. In the museums, people would cook, take care of things, clean, listen to music; discussions went on for days and even nights in order to achieve one thing: promoting dialogue with visitors and creating a sense of community. In the same vein, Nicolas Bourriaud also wrote in *Relational Aesthetics* (2002) that "it seems more pressing to invent possible relationships with our neighbors in the present than to bet on happier tomorrows."

Looking back at the three locations—Schweizergasse, Alemannengasse, and now Baslerstrasse in Allschwil—I recall which rooms art was allowed to take up space and flourish in, and which rooms we simply passed by. From cellars to utility rooms, bathrooms and attics, living rooms and kitchens to hallways and backyards—art was integrated everywhere. The only places we didn't visit were people's private

zusammenläuft. Dann bündelt sich die Energie. Gerade dann versuchen alle, rund um die Uhr präsent zu sein und ihren Beitrag zu leisten – sei es beim Aufhängen von Arbeiten, beim Beiseiteschieben von Teppichen und Regalen oder beim Kochen für die Vernissagegäste.

Man mag sich an die 1970er und 1980er Jahre erinnern, als Kunstschaffende erstmals zu neuen Grenzen aufbrachen und vor allem die unbekannten Welten dahinter erkundeten. In den Museen wurde gekocht, Fürsorge getragen, geputzt, Musik gehört; es wurde tage- und vor allem nächtelang diskutiert, um eben eines zu erreichen: den Austausch mit den Besucher*innen zu fördern und ein gemeinschaftliches Miteinander zu schaffen. In diesem Sinne schrieb auch Nicolas Bourriaud in *Relational Aesthetics* (2002), dass es „heute dringlicher scheint, hier und heute mögliche Beziehungen zu unseren Nachbarn zu knüpfen, als auf glückliche Zukünfte zu wetten."

Rückblickend auf die drei Orte – Schweizergasse, Alemannengasse und nun auch die Baslerstrasse in Allschwil – lasse ich die Erinnerungen daran Revue passieren, in welchen Zimmern die Kunst Raum ergreifen und gedeihen durfte und an welchen Räumen man vorbeiging. Von Kellern über Waschküchen, Badezimmer und Dachböden, Wohnzimmer und Küchen bis hin zu Fluren und Hinterhöfen – überall wurde Kunst integriert. Einzig vor den Privatgemächern

rooms. In this way, the public and the intimate are united under the same roof, and the private still manifests itself in public space—in toothbrushes, shelves, cups, glasses, and book displays—and mingles with the collective's understanding of art, which has subsequently expanded to include other artists: Madeleine Noraas, Vera Mühlebach, Jakub Andrzejewski, Ivan Mitrović, and Á. Birna Björnsdóttir.

And then there are other rooms that everyone has to themselves and which are not located in Palazzina Itself—such as a second home that they visit at weekends, or studios, which almost all of the artists at Palazzina also have. These spaces provide the tranquility and seclusion needed to further develop their own work.

But there is another new movement that the group has been experimenting with for some time: stepping outside. After a year and a half in Allschwil and incorporating the back garden into their projects, they are now moving out of the garden area altogether. Under the guidance of artist and architect Ester Alemayehu Hatle, as well as Emil Hvelplund Kristiansen and Jakub Andrzejewski, they created a mobile pavilion constructed out of a system of poles and brick-like elements made of hempcrete. This then traveled to major

wurde Halt gemacht. So vereint sich unter einem Dach das Öffentliche mit dem Intimen und Privaten, das sich doch auch im öffentlichen Raum manifestiert, in Zahnbürsten, Ablagen, Bechern, Tassen, Bücherauslagen, und vermischt sich mit dem Kunstverständnis des Kollektivs, das sich in der Folge noch um weitere Künstler*innen erweitert hat: Madeleine Noraas, Vera Mühlebach, Jakub Andrzejewski, Ivan Mitrović oder Á. Birna Björnsdóttir.

Und dann gibt es da noch andere Räume, die jede*r für sich allein hat und die sich nicht im eigentlichen Palazzina befinden – wie die zweite Heimat, die am Wochenende aufgesucht wird, oder die Atelierräume, die fast alle Kunstschaffenden des Palazzina zusätzlich nutzen. Diese Räume dienen dazu, das eigene Werk in aller Stille und in der nötigen Abgeschiedenheit weiterzuentwickeln.

Es gibt aber noch eine neue Bewegung, mit der die Gruppe seit einiger Zeit experimentiert: das Nach-aussen-Treten. Nach anderthalb Jahren in Allschwil und dem Einbezug des Hinterhofgartens in ihre Projekte geht es nun auch mal ganz hinaus aus dem Gartenumschwung. Unter Anleitung der Künstlerin und Architektin Ester Alemayehu Hatle sowie Emil Hvelplund Kristiansen und Jakub Andrzejewski entstand unter anderem ein mobiler Pavillon aus einem Stangensystem und ziegelartigen Elementen aus Hanfbeton. Dieser wanderte dann zu Grossevents wie dem Basel Social

events such as the Basel Social Club during Art Basel in 2023 and 2024 or served—in a different formation and with different materials—as a bar for the self-initiated performance event *Soft Collision* at the former post office in Allschwil; in the summer of 2023, it came to a rest on the neighboring Lindenplatz in Allschwil, where it became an exhibition space, action space, and meeting place for the local community.

It seems that venturing out into public space has become a new passion. This is not only due to the spatial restrictions of the existing locations, which can accommodate a lot, but do have space limitations. In addition, at its current, more village-like location, local residents frequently ask those involved what Palazzina is all about. Stepping out into the world therefore seems to be a logical consequence in order to answer this question directly through actions and art.

As I write this text, the group has once again set off to perform in a public space. For one day only, they can be found in a former post office in Allschwil. A large, empty space will be activated for an afternoon and evening by a performance program—a format that would not have been possible in the current building.

83

Club während der Art Basel 2023 und 2024 oder diente – in anderer Formation und mit anderem Material – als Bar beim selbstinitiierten Performance-Event *Soft Collision* in der ehemaligen Poststelle in Allschwil; im Sommer 2023 kam er auf dem benachbarten Lindenplatz in Allschwil zum Stehen, um dort Ausstellungsraum, Aktionsraum und Treffpunkt für die Bevölkerung zu werden.

Das Hinaustreten in die Öffentlichkeit hat sich als neue Lust entwickelt, so scheint es. Das liegt nicht nur an den räumlichen Beschränkungen der bestehenden Orte, die zwar vieles zulassen, aber eben auch Platzbeschränkungen haben. Zudem wurden am derzeitigen, eher dörflichen Standort häufiger Fragen aus dem Umfeld an die Beteiligten herangetragen, was das denn sei, das Palazzina. Der Schritt ins Aussen erscheint daher als logische Konsequenz, um diese Frage direkt durch Aktionen und Kunst zu beantworten.

Während ich diesen Text verfasse, hat sich die Gruppe erneut auf den Weg gemacht, um einen öffentlichen Ort zu bespielen. Für einen Tag sind sie in einer ehemaligen Poststation in Allschwil anzutreffen. Ein grosser, leerstehender Ort wird für einen Nachmittag und Abend durch ein Performanceprogramm aktiviert, um ein Format zu ermöglichen, das im bestehenden Haus so nicht realisierbar gewesen wäre.

My last question of the morning is whether they think about the future at all—that is, beyond one annual program to the next? After all, a lot of things have changed for them over the years. They almost all belong to the same generation, living here as couples, as (future) families, or even as friends. Nevertheless, they frequently leave this place for varying periods of time—whether for residencies in Europe or South America, to travel, or to devote themselves more intensively to their own work for a while. At certain points they also have to work more in order to earn a living.

"Some of us want to stay together no matter what," says Noemi Pfister, obviously voicing everyone's wish, even though life will take its own course. She has noticed that there can be a great longing for those who are temporarily absent, such as the family who spent a year in Rome and then returned to the house with their child. For others, however, adds Ines Tondar, Basel is perhaps only a stopover and it is therefore perfectly natural for people to move on. Maybe, according to Simone Holliger, it is important for a certain core to remain, one that forms the starting point for everything and does not get lost. This prevents the group from becoming too static.

84

Denken sie denn, so meine letzte Frage an diesem Vormittag, auch bisweilen in die Zukunft – also viel weiter als nur von einem Jahresprogramm zum nächsten? Schliesslich hat sich in der Zwischenzeit einiges bei ihnen getan. Sie gehören zwar fast alle derselben Generation an, leben hier als Paar, als (werdende) Familie oder eben in Freundschaft zusammen. Dennoch verlassen sie diesen Ort immer wieder für kürzere oder längere Zeit – sei es für Residencies in Europa oder Südamerika, um zu reisen oder um sich für kürzere oder längere Zeit noch intensiver dem eigenen Schaffen zu widmen. Auch muss hier und dort mehr gearbeitet werden, um den Lebensunterhalt zu bestreiten.

„Einige von uns möchten in jedem Fall zusammenbleiben", so Noemi Pfister, die damit offensichtlich den Wunsch aller formuliert, selbst wenn das Leben seinen Gang geht. Sie habe festgestellt, dass eine grosse Sehnsucht nach denjenigen entstehen könne, die vorübergehend abwesend sind, etwa nach der Familie, die ein Jahr in Rom verbracht hat und dann mit ihrem Kind wieder in das Haus zurückgekehrt ist. Für andere wiederum, so fügt Ines Tondar hinzu, sei Basel vielleicht nur eine Zwischenstation, und es sei daher legitim, dass man weiterziehe. Vielleicht, so Simone Holliger, sei es wichtig, dass stets ein gewisser Kern erhalten bleibe, von dem alles ausgehe und

Perhaps, I think as I leave the building, it would be more accurate to speak of a common spark that is kindled by the various people in the collective—above all through a shared interest in art, togetherness, and the desire not only to carry this fire within the group, but also to take it out and share it with the world. Perhaps this is what has characterized Palazzina since it was founded five years ago and what continues to define it. And if things keep going the way they are, this flame will probably continue to burn brightly for a few more years to come.

INES GOLDBACH has been the director and curator of the Kunsthaus Baselland since 2013 and has already realized over 100 exhibitions. She played a pivotal role in the construction of the new Kunsthaus in Basel's Dreispitz area. The art historian wrote her thesis on the artist Jannis Kounellis and Arte Povera. She subsequently spent many years working as a curator for the Raussmüller Collection at the Hallen für Neue Kunst Schaffhausen and as a lecturer at the Institute of Art History at the University of Freiburg i. Br. In 2024, the French government awarded Ines Goldbach the *Chevalier de l'Ordre des Arts et Lettres*.

85

der sich nicht verliere. So vermeide man es, zu einer zu festgefahrenen Gruppe zu werden.

Vielleicht, so überlege ich beim Verlassen des Hauses, liesse sich eher von einem gemeinsamen Funken sprechen, der sich bei den verschiedenen Menschen des Kollektivs entzündet – vor allem durch das gemeinsame Interesse an der Kunst, das Miteinander und den Wunsch, dieses Feuer nicht nur im Miteinander zu tragen, sondern es auch nach aussen zu tragen und zu teilen. Vielleicht ist es das, was das Palazzina seit seiner Gründung vor fünf Jahren auszeichnet und was es weiterschreibt. Und wenn es so weitergeht, wird die Flamme wohl noch einige Jahre famos weiterlodern.

INES GOLDBACH ist seit 2013 Direktorin des Kunsthaus Baselland und kuratierte bereits über 100 Ausstellungen. Sie begleitete massgeblich den Neubau des Kunsthaus Baselland auf dem Dreispitz. Goldbach wurde über den Künstler Jannis Kounellis und die Arte Povera promoviert, arbeitete langjährig als Kuratorin an den Hallen für Neue Kunst Schaffhausen für die Raussmüller Collection sowie als Lehrbeauftragte am Kunsthistorischen Institut der Universität Freiburg i. Br. Im Jahr 2024 wurde sie mit dem *Chevalier de l'Ordre des Arts et Lettres* ausgezeichnet.

Cassiane C. Pfund

A Visit to Palazzina

Exhibition
Space   ⟨∿⟩   Guest Room

The artist-run space Palazzina is now located at Baslerstrasse 321, 4123 Allschwil. I didn't take any photos. To remember, I listen. To the sounds of the house, the creaking, the voices: V.'s, N.'s, N.'s, mine, our bodies moving through the rooms, meeting in the first-floor kitchen—there are several of them, and an exponential number of fridges—then sitting down around the table. This is just as much a ghostly reconstruction based on the superimposition of notes, sounds, memories, associations, and impressions as it is a journey with all its detours and surprises. Time is stretched. A new fiction of place.

▲   ▼

Une Visite à Palazzina

Espace d'expo ⟷ Chambre d'Amiexs

L'artist run space Palazzina est aujourd'hui situé Baslerstrasse 321, 4123 Allschwil. Je n'ai pris aucune photo. Pour
me remémorer, j'écoute. Les bruits de la maison, les craque-
ments, les voix : celles de V., N., N., la mienne, nos corps
parcourant les pièces, réunis dans la cuisine du 1er étage –
il y en a plusieurs, et un nombre de frigos exponentiel –
puis s'installant à table. Il est autant question d'une reconstitution fantomatique reposant sur la superposition de
notes, de sons, de souvenirs, d'associations et d'impressions,
que d'un cheminement avec ses détours et ses imprévus.
Un temps étiré. Une nouvelle fiction des lieux.

▲   ▼

Attic

(5.)

Under the roof are three bedrooms and a bathroom. A ceramic telephone. In summer, it gets really hot! T., the child of the house, lives here. Arrangements for events and exhibitions are discussed in advance. V. takes out a bunch of keys. A trapdoor in the ceiling squeaks open; a staircase unfolds before us. There's never been too many exhibitions up there. There was a projection there once. But now there's so much stuff…

When I search through the website archives later, I will learn that the projected work was *Dous faros (Insua e Roncudo)* by Lara and Noa Castro.[1] The description informs me that it "reflects on the etymology of the word 'copla' and the ideas it conveys of togetherness, encounters, or unions, but also poetic associations and emergences of memory and dreams in very simple quotidian things."[2] Without having seen it, the video seems to have found in Palazzina a resonance chamber, an anchor point, a possible extension. As my visit progresses, the walls soften and the expected boundaries unravel: the customary separation between "exhibition space" and "domestic space" probably never existed here. The home remains, intertwined. V. closes the door. We go back down a floor.

1   *Dous Faros (Insua e Roncudo)* was presented as part of *Parallel-montage ~ Palazzina #18* from 3–19.3.2023.
2   Excerpt from the *Parallelmontage* brochure, Palazzina, March 2023.

Attique

(5.)

Sous le toit, trois chambres et une salle de bain. Un téléphone en céramique. En été il fait vraiment chaud! Ici vit T., l'enfant de la maison. Des aménagements sont discutés en amont des événements et des expositions. V. sort un trousseau de clés. Une porte dans le plafond s'ouvre en grinçant, des escaliers se déploient. On n'a jamais trop fait d'expo là-haut. Une fois, il y a eu une projection. Mais maintenant, on a tellement d'affaires…

En fouillant dans les archives du site Internet, j'apprendrai que l'œuvre projetée était: *Dous faros (Insua e Roncudo)* de Lara et Noa Castro[1]. Le descriptif m'informe qu'elle « réfléchit à l'étymologie du mot ‹ copla › (fr. ‹ couplet ›) et les idées qu'il véhicule autour de l'unité, de l'être ensemble ou de l'union, mais aussi d'associations poétiques et d'émergences de la mémoire et du rêve dans des choses quotidiennes très simples. »[2] Sans en avoir fait l'expérience, la vidéo semble avoir trouvé en Palazzina une caisse de résonance; un point d'ancrage, une possible prolongation. À mesure de la visite, les murs ramollissent, les frontières attendues se brouillent: la séparation d'usage entre « espace d'exposition » et « espace domestique » n'a sans doute jamais eu lieu. Le foyer demeure, intriqué. V. ferme la porte. On redescend d'un étage.

1   *Dous Faros (Insua e Roncudo)* a été présenté dans le cadre de *Parallelmontage ~ Palazzina #18*, du 3.3. au 19.3.2023.

2   Extrait tiré de la brochure de *Parallelmontage*, Palazzina, mars 2023.

Staircase

▲

▼

(4.)
Creeaak, creeaak, creeaak…

(6.)
On the staircase, you can see the previous locations of an installation by Vicente Lesser Gutierrez, *Nexo*.[3]

Second floor

(0.)
Between my drowsiness and the sleep still stuck to my eyes, I don't know how long I was asleep for.

(7.)
You're already familiar with this bit, the exhibition space and the reception area. V.'s room is over there, but she's in Paris. The kitchen on this floor is used when you need some quiet time to yourself. As I become more familiar with these spaces, where exactly is "Palazzina"? On the face of it, the exhibition space on the second floor. However, its continuous overflow makes it closely interwoven with the whole building: no longer an "annex," it creates space for a labyrinthine field of exploration, a polyphony of voices and nooks and crannies. At the moment, we're in the interval between the end of dismantling one exhibition and the beginning of installing the next. The adaptation of spaces seems organic; sometimes they retain hints of their past or a temporarily suspended use. The guest room[a] is filled with packaged ceramic works, ready for collection. Last year, Ingo Niermann installed the mattress—the

---

3   *Nexo* was presented as part of *Counter Loopholes ~ Palazzina #20*, 26.5–8.7.2023.

Cage d'escalier

▲   ▼

(4.)
Craaac, Craaac
Craaac…

(6.)
Dans la cage d'escalier, les emplacements passés d'une installation de Vicente Lesser Gutierrez, *Nexo*.[3]

2ème étage

(0.)
Entre l'écœurement et le sommeil encore collé à mes yeux, j'ignore combien de temps j'ai dormi.

(7.)
Ça tu connais maintenant, c'est la salle d'expo, et l'accueil. Là, c'est la chambre de V., mais elle est à Paris. À cet étage, la cuisine est utilisée lorsque le besoin de se retrouver avec soi-même appelle au calme. Si les lieux me sont de plus en plus familiers, que désigne « Palazzina » ? A priori, l'espace d'exposition situé au deuxième étage. Pourtant, son débordement continu le fond intimement à l'ensemble : « l'annexe » abolie, elle laisse place à un champ d'explo-ration labyrinthique, une polyphonie de voix et de recoins. En ce moment, on évolue dans cet intervalle entre fin de démontage et début de montage. L'adaptation des espaces semble organique, conservant quelquefois les indices d'un usage passé ou temporairement suspendu. La chambre d'amiexs[a] abrite des œuvres en céramique emballées, prêtes à être récupérées. L'année dernière, Ingo Niermann

3   *Nexo* a été présenté dans le cadre de *Counter Loopholes ~ Palazzina #20*, 26.5. au 8.7.2023.

one I slept on—to allow the audience to relax and watch his film *Deutsch Süd-Ost*.[4] I enjoy reading these gestures or little games of presence and absence as signs of this entanglement. If the identity of Palazzina is revealed *in relation to*, blending home with the collective management of an art space and exhibitions within the same building, hospitality[b] is at the heart of its structure.

a. There is something intimate about sharing where you sleep: the increased proximity or the bringing together of bodies, each plunged into a state of altered consciousness (except in the case of insomnia or sleep disorders); the unveiling of a frank vulnerability. The "guest room" as a potential place of welcome, whether temporary or permanent, flexible or something "extra," intrigues me. There are as many ways of being connected, as many modes of friendship, as there are nuances, subtle layers that, in small increments, reveal a closeness that is intimately linked to the space between two distinct entities: the genesis of a shared story that is in the process of being written. Suddenly, I turn my attention to these intervening spaces, this "in-between." It has the capacity to expand, to relax, to distend, creating as much as it diminishes (itself) to the point of disappearance. Unmeasurable, yet indexical, perhaps it serves to render a certain sensation tangible: the synchronization of breaths, the softening of gazes and, for an unpredictable length of time, the emergence of a mutual understanding. Part of this understanding comes from recognizing and listening to the various ways in which the two—simultaneously other and familiar—elements intersect.

b. In French, the term "hôte" (host) is used to mean both "the person who receives someone" and "the person who is being received." It refers as much to the action of welcoming and giving as to that of visiting and receiving, linking two interdependent practices to the same space. At Palazzina, I sleep in the guest room.[c] This room turns out to be the "main" exhibition room: white walls, antique floor, a single east-facing window. I like the idea of a chameleon-like surface that recounts what it has experienced through a series of clues—wear and tear, patina, marks, filled-in holes, shared memories. What if this were a kind of stratification? Stratification, when it occurs, can serve to show us things, building up successive layers to form clusters of stories that are most often accessed in fragments. Our bodies memorize this experience and then carry the memories further. I once read that our body memories are informed by the previous fourteen generations. Our cells contain an invisible legacy, other lives whose contribution to

4   *Deutsch Süd-Ost* was presented as part of *Counter Loopholes ~ Palazzina #20* from 26.5–8.7.2023.

avait installé le matelas – sur lequel j'ai dormi – permettant
au public de se déposer pour visionner son film *Deutsch
Süd-Ost*[4]. Je m'amuse à lire ces gestes ou menus jeux de
présences-absences comme les signes de cette intrication.
Si Palazzina se révèle en *relation à*, mêlant foyer, gestion
collective d'un espace d'art et expositions au sein d'un même
édifice, l'hospitalité[b] s'inscrit au cœur de sa structure.

 a. Partager son sommeil participe d'une certaine intimité :
l'accroissement d'une contiguïté, soit le rapprochement
de corps chacun plongé dans un état de conscience altérée
(sauf insomnie, et troubles du sommeil) ; le dévoilement
d'une vulnérabilité sans fard. La « chambre d'amiexs » en
tant que lieu d'accueil possible, intermittent ou à temps plein,
modulable ou « en sus », m'intrigue. Il existe autant de
manières d'être en lien, de modes amicaux que de nuances,
des fines strates qui, par touches, racontent une proximité –
indissociable de l'espace entre deux entités distinctes :
la genèse d'une histoire commune en cours d'écriture.
Soudain, je pose mon attention sur ces interstices, cet
« entre ». Il a la capacité de s'étendre, de se détendre,
de se distendre, faisant advenir autant qu'il (s')amenuise,
jusqu'à faire disparaître. Non mesurable, malgré tout
indiciel, il rend manifeste, peut-être, une sensation : l'accor-
dage des respirations, l'adoucissement du regard et, pour
une durée toujours imprédictible, l'émergence d'une
compréhension mutuelle. Cette compréhension s'inscrit en
partie dans la reconnaissance et l'écoute de découpages
qui, tout en étant à la fois autres et familiers, se rencontrent.

 b. En français, le terme « hôte » désigne à la fois
« la personne qui reçoit » et « celle qui est reçue ». Il dit
autant l'action d'accueillir et de donner que celle de visiter
et de recevoir, liant deux pratiques interdépendantes
à un même espace. À Palazzina, je dors dans la chambre
d'amiexs[c]. Cette pièce se révèle être la salle « principale »
d'exposition : murs blancs, plancher ancien, unique
fenêtre orientation est. J'aime bien l'idée d'une surface
caméléon qui raconte, au travers d'une collection d'indices –
l'usure, la patine, les marques, les trous rebouchés, les
souvenirs partagés – ce par quoi elle a été traversée. Et s'il
était question de stratification ? Lorsqu'elle se produit,
la stratification agit tel un révélateur, formant, par la constitution de couches successives, des faisceaux d'histoires
auxquelles l'on accède le plus souvent par bribes. Leur
expérience est mémorisée par les corps qui en poussent les
mémoires plus loin. J'ai lu une fois que nos mémoires

4 *Deutsch Süd-Ost* a été présenté dans le cadre de *Counter Loopholes ~ Palazzina #20*, 26.5. au 8.7.2023.

shaping our own is still unknown. Would lifting all the layers of a place enable us to go all the way back to the formation of the earth, then of the universe, right back to the one before the one we're currently floating in?

How far back is it possible to go?

Sea turtles return to nest on the beach where they were born, sometimes traveling thousands of kilometers. They remember, or re-remember. When exactly are they remembering?

c. The history of the guest room at Villa Noailles in Hyères (France) resonates with that of Palazzina, although there is a certain contextual difference. Dutch architect Sybold van Ravesteyn designed the entire layout of the room in Hyères—wood and metal furniture painted in different colors—and oversaw its realization between 1925 and 1926.[5] Dedicated to creation and a certain emulation of the artistic and literary avant-garde, the villa regularly welcomed friends of the family. Listed as a historic monument and now an arts center, it has undergone renovation several times. Since summer 2023, as part of the building's centenary celebrations, the guest room on the second floor is being reconstructed on the basis of archival documents (photographs, plans, drawings, letters, etc.) and the only remaining armchair.[6] However, as a heritage site that is open to the public, its original function is lost and the room will apparently no longer be inhabited or habitable. While Palazzina's operations differ from those of Villa Noailles in this regard, the former being based on a collective way of life supported by its inhabitants, they both address, from very different points, the need for friendship. Often overlooked in relation to creative work, and even more so when it comes to inter-species encounters, these stories, undoubtedly deemed too insignificant, nonetheless form the delicate foundations of all the others. In the same vein, if weaving reflects the process of its creation, it is partly in this return to a rhythm anchored in a cyclical temporality with a deep spatial connection, freed from the pressures of consumption, that a new realm of possibility emerges, one in which finished products and final images once again become attempts, myths of "personal success," love stories, and plural narratives. An ever-evolving web of active learning and communication.

5   Mathilde Wagman and Sébastien Thème, "La villa Noailles a 100 ans," *Bienvenue au Club,* published by France Culture, August 2, 2023, online.
6   Monique Teunissen, "Sybold van Ravesteyn: La reconstitution de la chambre d'amis (1925–26)," *Design Parade Hyères 2023* (2023).

corporelles seraient informées par les quatorze générations précédentes. Nos cellules contiendraient un legs invisible, d'autres vies dont on ne sait encore très bien comment elles contribuent à façonner les nôtres.

Est-ce que soulever toutes les couches d'un lieu permettrait de revenir à la formation de la Terre, puis de l'univers, jusqu'à celui-là même avant celui dans lequel nous flottons ?

Jusqu'où est-il possible de remonter ?

Les tortues de mer retournent nicher à la plage qui les a vues naître, parcourant quelquefois plusieurs milliers de kilomètres. Elles se souviennent ou se ressouviennent. Depuis quand savent-elles ?

c. L'histoire de *La chambre d'amis* de la villa Noailles, à Hyères (France), résonne, non sans un décalage notamment contextuel, avec Palazzina. L'architecte hollandais Sybold van Ravesteyn en dessine l'aménagement complet – des meubles en bois et en métal peints de différentes couleurs – puis en assure la réalisation entre 1925 et 1926.[5] La maison, dédiée à la création et à une certaine émulation de l'avant-garde artistique et littéraire, accueillait régulièrement des amiexs de la famille. Classée monument historique, désormais centre d'art, elle a connu plusieurs cycles de rénovation. Dans le cadre du centenaire de l'édifice, et depuis l'été 2023, *la chambre d'amis* située au deuxième étage est en cours de reconstitution à partir de documents d'archive (photographies, plans, dessins, courriers…) et de l'unique fauteuil restant.[6] Au prix d'une désactivation de sa fonction initiale, en tant que patrimoine exposé, elle ne sera a priori plus ni habitée ni habitable. Si bien sûr le fonctionnement de Palazzina diverge vis-à-vis de celui de la villa Noailles, le premier reposant sur une vie en collectif portée par ses habitantexs, elles adressent, depuis un endroit autrement situé, la nécessité du lien d'amitié. Souvent invisibilisées dans un rapport à la création, et plus encore lorsqu'il s'agit de rencontres interespèces, ces histoires, sans doute jugées trop minuscules, constituent pourtant les fondations sensibles de toutes les autres. En ce sens, si le tissage dit son processus, c'est en partie dans le retour à un rythme lui-même ancré dans une temporalité cyclique et en lien profond avec les lieux, départi d'une pression de consommation, que s'ouvre un possible au sein duquel les produits finis et les images finales redeviennent des tentatives, les mythes de « réussite

5   Mathilde Wagman et Sébastien Thème, « La villa Noailles a 100 ans », *Bienvenue au Club*, France Culture, 2 août 2023, en ligne.

6   Monique Teunissen, « Sybold van Ravesteyn. La reconstitution de la chambre d'amis (1925-1926) », *Design Parade Hyères 2023* (2023).

Staircase

<table>
<tr><td>▲</td><td>▼</td></tr>
</table>

(3.)
Creeaak, creeaak, creeaak…
V. bounds down the stairs at top speed.

(1.)
It all starts with *Stories from the City, Stories from the Sea*,[7] a PJ Harvey album, and a plastic dinosaur. The sound of "This Is Love" playing gets louder and louder as we get closer to the living room on the first floor. It's the summer break at the moment, and Palazzina is running at a slower pace.

(8.)
They're so high, I can hardly keep up … The steps creeaak.

---

7   PJ Harvey, *Stories from the City, Stories from the Sea*, produced and performed by PJ Harvey, Rob Ellis, and Mick Harvey, Island Records, 2000.

personnelle », des histoires d'amour et des récits pluriels. Une toile en cours parcourue d'apprentissages et de transmissions vivantes.

Cage d'escalier

▲   ▼

(3.)
Craaac, Craaac Craaac…
V. sautille, enjambe les marches à toute vitesse.

(1.)
Tout commence par *Stories from the City, stories from the sea*,[7] un disque de PJ Harvey, et un dinosaure en plastique. *This is love* de plus en plus fort dans l'enregistreur à mesure que le salon situé au premier étage se rapproche. En ce moment, c'est la pause estivale, Palazzina est au ralenti.

(8.)
Elles sont hautes, j'ai de la peine à suivre… Craaac, les marches.

7   PJ Harvey, *Stories from the City, Stories from the Sea*, Island Records, 2000. Produit et interprété par PJ Harvey, Rob Ellis et Mick Harvey.

First floor

(2.)
V. is making potato salad with pickles ♡. It's after 5 pm. Time for a tour of the house.

(9.)
Now, *Horses in My Dreams* is playing. In the background, the floor plays a different rhythm. A shoe rack and a large mirror are on the threshold. The apartment, which is structured along the same lines as the ground and second floors, has also had its front door removed: there is an east-facing dining room with two large windows, a shelf on the back wall displaying a collection of assorted wine glasses, then a comfortable living room with a soon-to-be-absent sofa and a bookcase with rows of books. The ones on an angle indicate that this empty space was once occupied, their fragile equilibrium signaling the departure of a housemate. On the right, as you leave the living room, is another bedroom: it belongs to I. We pass through the kitchen into a glazed west-facing corridor; I suddenly picture an indoor balcony or a winter garden. Last spring, this same corridor hosted *Hi <3 look at this thing that I love!*,[8] a sound piece by Jennifer Merlyn Scherler; V. wrote a text based on the artist's written description of the work[9] that I find really moving. Here's an excerpt: "Accumulation here is directly connected to the impossibility and tristesse of containing the things accumulated in one single person or household—not only because (fictional) worlds are infinite—and thus emphasizes the importance of holding knowledge together."[10] Perhaps description is a response to this *tristesse*: an arbitrary desire to share the places and experiences of this world perceived through the—always incomplete—process of transformation that is translation, despite its inability to fully retrace their contours. When words are used to bring people together, they have the capacity to establish points of reference, a foundation on which shared dreams can be built. Palazzina may well be one of these foundations. I listen to her telling me about it. On the right is a bathroom with a toilet. Opposite, a study. Through the window, below, is a courtyard surrounded by trees, a hammock, the roof of a garden shed.

8   *Hi <3 look at this thing that I love!* was presented as part of *Scarecrows Don't Talk ~ Palazzina #24* from 31.5–7.7.2024.
9   Jennifer Merlyn Scherler is inspired by the research work of Nancy Baym.
10   Excerpt from the exhibition text for *Scarecrows Don't Talk* by Vera Mühlebach (2024).

1er étage

(2.)
V. prépare une salade de pommes de terre aux cornichons ♡.
Il est 17 heures passées. L'heure du tour de la maison.

(9.)
À présent, *Horses in my dreams.* En arrière-fond, le plancher
joue un autre rythme. Sur le seuil, un meuble à chaussures,
un large miroir. L'appartement est structuré sur le modèle de
celui du rez-de-chaussée et du deuxième étage, dont
la porte d'entrée a elle aussi été retirée : une salle à manger
orientation est avec deux larges fenêtres, et adossée au
mur du fond, une étagère exhibant sa collection de verres
multiformes à pied, puis un salon confortable avec un
sofa bientôt absent comprenant une bibliothèque aux livres
alignés. Ceux en biais indiquent l'espace vide autrefois
occupé, signalant depuis leur point d'équilibre fragile,
le départ d'une colocataire. À droite en sortant du salon, une
autre chambre à coucher : c'est I. qui vit là. On emprunte la
cuisine pour rejoindre un couloir vitré orienté ouest ; je
visualise soudain un balcon d'intérieur ou un jardin d'hiver.
Le printemps dernier, ce même couloir a hébergé *Hi <3
look at this thing that I love!*,[8] une pièce sonore de Jennifer
Merlyn Scherler à propos de laquelle V. a écrit un texte
à partir d'une description de l'œuvre rédigée par l'artiste [9]
qui me touche. En voici un extrait : « L'accumulation est ici
directement liée à l'impossibilité et à la tristesse de contenir
les choses accumulées par une seule personne ou un
seul foyer – non seulement parce que les mondes (fictifs) sont
infinis – mais aussi parce qu'il est important de cultiver
les connaissances ensemble. »[10] Peut-être la description
s'affaire-t-elle en réponse à cette tristesse : une velléité
arbitraire de partager des lieux et vécus du monde ressentis
au travers du processus de transformation – toujours partiel –
qu'est la traduction… et ce en dépit de son impossibilité
à retracer les contours tout à fait. Quand le recours aux mots
voue à rassembler, ces derniers ont la capacité d'instaurer
des repères, un socle à partir duquel se sédimentent des
rêves communs. Palazzina est peut-être l'un de ces socles.
Je l'écoute me raconter. Sur la droite, une salle de bain

8   *Hi <3 look at this thing that I love!* a été présenté dans le cadre de
     Scarecrows Don't Talk ~ Palazzina #24, du 31.5. au 7.7.2024.
9   Jennifer Merlyn Scherler s'inspire du travail de recherche de Nancy
     Baym.
10   Extrait tiré du texte d'exposition de *Scarecrows Don't Talk*, Vera
     Mühlebach, 2024.

(17.)
We're back in the kitchen. The tour of the house is finished;
back to preparing tonight's meal. N. and N. join us.

Staircase

▲

(16.)
A stomach rumbles.

▼

(10.)
V. rushes rather than bounds
down the stairs now.

avec WC. En face, un cabinet. Par la fenêtre, en contrebas, une cour entourée d'arbres, un hamac, le toit d'une cabane de jardin.

(17.)
À nouveau bis, la cuisine. Le tour de la maison se termine. On reprend la préparation du repas de ce soir, N. et N. nous rejoignent.

Cage d'escalier

▲

(16.)
Un ventre gargouille.

▼

(10.)
V. ne sautille plus, dévale.

Ground floor

(courtyard and entrance hall)

(11.)
This is the last floor, that's M.'s room, that one's B.'s, and that one's mine. There's not much light. I should buy a UV lamp for my plants . . . Outside, feet are sticking out of the hammock. For a moment, it makes you think of a sculpture with false feet, giving the impression of a hammock that's always occupied. The door to the courtyard opens with difficulty. There have been performances in the glazed corridor of the ground-floor apartment, with the windows open and the audience outside. One of these was during the first vernissage at this address [11] with Livio Casanova, Lorraine Baylac, and LapTopRadio in September 2022 and another was Ana Bălan's concert in January 2024. The garden shed houses three other fridges, which are used to store drinks for the bar. V. tells me about G., the squirrel who feeds by climbing the hazel tree. We retrace our steps, the garden door slams shut, we re-enter the kitchen, and finally the entrance hall.

(12.)
Opposite the staircase are a few flyers within reach, two T-shirts designed by Marius Margot hanging on the wall, and a long corridor. It leads to the main door. I wonder if the circulation between the different rooms and floors of this house doesn't contribute to this feeling of openness. The spatial biographies of the people who live, exhibit, visit, stick around, or just pass through here. A choreography that is being constantly renewed. How do you organize an environment in which "work," "welcoming the public," and "domestic space" coexist? How do you handle slowing down?

---

11   The opening of Palazzina at its current address was held on 1.9.2022 to mark the launch of *Façade: Hello Baslerstrasse! ~ Palazzina #16* from 1–18.9.2022.

Rez-de-chaussée

(cour + hall d'entrée)

(11.)
Ici, c'est le dernier étage, la chambre de M., là c'est B., et là c'est moi. Il n'y a pas beaucoup de lumière. Je devrais acheter une lampe UV pour mes plantes… Dehors, des pieds sortent du hamac. On songe un instant à une sculpture de faux pieds laissant croire à un hamac toujours occupé. La porte menant à la cour s'ouvre, non sans peine. Des performances se sont déroulées dans le couloir vitré de l'appartement du rez-de-chaussée, les fenêtres ouvertes, le public installé à l'extérieur. C'était lors du premier vernissage à cette adresse[11] avec Livio Casanova, Lorraine Baylac et LapTopRadio, en septembre 2022, ou encore lors du concert d'Ana Bălan en janvier 2024. La cabane de jardin abrite trois autres frigos, ils servent à stocker les boissons pour le bar. V. me parle de G., l'écureuil qui se nourrit en grimpant dans le noisetier. On rebrousse chemin, la porte du jardin claque, à nouveau la cuisine, enfin, le hall d'entrée.

(12.)
Face à la cage d'escalier, quelques flyers à portée, deux t-shirts créés par Marius Margot suspendus au mur, un long couloir. Il conduit à la porte principale. Je me demande si la circulation entre les différentes pièces et étages de cette maison ne participe pas de ce sentiment d'ouverture. Les biographies spatiales de celleux qui y vivent, exposent, visitent, s'attardent, ne font que passer. Une chorégraphie constamment renouvelée. Comment s'organise un environnement au sein duquel cohabitent « travail », « accueil d'un public » et « espace domestique » ? Comment se soigne le ralentissement ?

11   Le vernissage de Palazzina à la présente adresse s'est tenu le 1.9.2022 à l'occasion de *Façade: Hello Baslerstrasse! ~ Palazzina #16*, du 1.9. au 18.9.2022.

Staircase

▲　　　　　　　　▼

(15.)
The steps support our hypotheses. Other questions are eagerly waiting to be asked.

(13.)
The concrete steps don't creak under our feet. In socks, mine can feel a colder draught. We continue our descent.

Basement

(14.)
So now we're in the basement. There's lots of stuff. There is a workshop with tools, which is great for building or organizing things around the house! The utility room produces a slight echo. There is underwear hanging up, and you can hear the faint clacking of clothespins as they close against the fabric pressed onto the line. I pushed the microphone as close to them as possible. There was once a video by Leevi Toija titled *On Illumination and Disposition* [12] in the space in the middle. Because it's so dark, it worked very well in this environment: "a lamp in the exhibition space." [13] At the top of the stairs is a screen with a worm singing in auto-tune: *Ditch me—Worm Soliloquy* by Rhona Mühlebach. [14] Or *Fonte*, a sculpture by Paulo Wirz. [15] Incidentally, I learned yesterday—N. told me because I wasn't there—that a duct runs all the way through the house; someone played sound through it from the roof.

12　*On Illumination and Disposition* was presented as part of *Parallel-montage ~ Palazzina #18* from 3–19.3.2023.
13　Excerpt from the *Parallelmontage* brochure, Palazzina, March 2023.
14　*Ditch me—Worm Soliloquy* was presented as part of *Scarecrows Don't Talk ~ Palazzina #24* from 31.5–7.7.2024.
15　*Fonte* was presented as part of *The Day Before ~ Palazzina #19* from 14.4–7.5.2023.

Cage d'escalier

▲

▼

(15.)
Les marches soutiennent nos hypothèses. D'autres questions se réjouissent d'advenir.

(13.)
Les marches en béton ne craquent pas sous les pieds En chaussettes, les miens éprouvent un courant d'air plus froid. On poursuit la descente.

Cave

(14.)
Donc là, on est à la cave. Il y a beaucoup de trucs. Ici, un atelier avec des outils. Pour des questions de construction ou d'arrangement dans la maison, c'est super ! La buanderie produit un léger écho. Les culottes se suspendent, on entend les pinces à linge et leur clappement sourd au moment de se refermer sur le tissu pressé contre la corde. J'ai collé le micro au plus près. Une fois, dans l'espace du milieu, une vidéo de Leevi Toija *On illumination and Disposition*.[12] Parce qu'il fait bien sombre, ça marchait très bien avec l'environnement : « une lampe dans l'espace d'exposition. »[13] En haut des escaliers, un écran avec un ver qui chantait en auto-tune : *Ditch me – Worm Soliloquy* de Rhona Mühlebach.[14] Ou encore *Fonte*, une sculpture de Paulo Wirz.[15] D'ailleurs, j'ai appris hier – N. me l'a raconté car je n'étais pas là – qu'un conduit traverse toute la maison ;

12 *On Illumination and Disposition* a été présenté dans le cadre de *Parallelmontage ~ Palazzina #18*, du 3.3. au 19.3.2023.
13 Extrait tiré de la brochure de *Parallelmontage*, Palazzina, mars 2023.
14 *Ditch me – Worm Soliloquy* a été présenté dans le cadre de *Scarecrows Don't Talk ~ Palazzina #24*, du 31.5. au 7.7.2024.
15 *Fonte* a été présenté dans le cadre de *The Day Before ~ Palazzina #19*, du 14.4. au 7.5.2023.

I'd love to see artists and architects invited to interrogate and make direct interventions *in* structures and built spaces. Listening to V. again, I can't help but wonder if there isn't a link with the compartmentalization of practices, if categories don't end up hindering our ability to spontaneously imagine hybrid, mutant, liquid forms, our urge to escape scripts and prefabricated habits. Not to (re)produce them, but rather to unblock their clogged mechanisms. How can we coexist differently with what already exists? How can we override the programming of our own imaginative reflexes? The washing machine opens, V. starts a new load. We go back upstairs.

Between writing, art, research, and poetry, CASSIANE C. PFUND is passionate about hybrid, intersecting practices. Using words as a starting point, they explore other media such as performance, installation, and publishing as sculptures and collective experiences of transmission. Their aim is to open up spaces where people can meet, exchange stories, feel their emotions, and raise questions.

quelqu'un y a diffusé du son depuis le toit. J'aimerais bien
que l'on invite des artistexs et des architectexs qui inter-
viennent directement *sur*, et interrogent les structures, les
espaces bâtis. En réécoutant V., je me demande s'il n'y
a pas un lien avec le cloisonnement des pratiques. Si les
catégories ne finissent pas par nuire à notre capacité
a imaginer spontanément des formes hybrides, mutantes,
liquides, autant d'élans pour échapper aux scripts et aux
habitudes préfabriquées. Non pour en (re)produire, plutôt
pour en décongestionner les mécanismes agglutinés.
Comment coexister autrement avec ce qui existe déjà ?
Comment déjouer l'encodage de nos propres réflexes
imaginatifs ? La machine à laver s'ouvre, V. en lance une
nouvelle. On remonte.

Entre écriture, art, recherche et poésie, CASSIANE C. PFUND se passionne
pour les pratiques hybrides, à l'intersection. Utilisant les mots comme
point de départ, ses explorations convoquent d'autres médiums tels que
la performance, l'installation et la publication comme sculpture et
expérience de transmission. Son souhait est d'ouvrir des espaces au sein
desquels se rencontrer, échanger des histoires, ressentir ses émotions
et soulever des questions.

Hosting

Hosten

Nora Joung

On the subject of showing exhibitions in your living space, art, Switzerland, and being sociable, allow me to derail this text before it has even begun by recounting a story. Years ago, a friend approached me, wanting to exhibit in my run-down, cold, and cheap rental apartment. I was immediately skeptical. I already ran one artist-run exhibition space; I didn't feel the need to run two. I don't like people wearing shoes in my home any more than I like removing mine in an exhibition space. I didn't entirely understand my friend's motives. I couldn't imagine how much courage you needed to want to insert yourself and your art into somebody else's home. I am staunchly private. I didn't need people to know that I lived in squalor, what the contents of my fridge were, or how many books by Simone Weil I obsessively hoarded. But I relented. Hospitality is what makes culture possible, after all. The artist and their spouse came with a truckload of unfinished artworks on the morning of the opening. As my hairline began to tingle, they started taking down the numerous works that were already in my possession and stashing them in my bedroom. I made a leap of faith and left the apartment to go to work. If my memory serves me right, my friend contacted me

109

Ich möchte diesen Text über Ausstellungen in den eigenen vier Wänden, über Kunst, die Schweiz und Geselligkeit mit einer etwas abwegigen Anekdote einleiten. Vor einigen Jahren wandte sich ein Freund an mich, der in meiner heruntergekommenen, kalten und schäbigen Mietwohnung ausstellen wollte. Zunächst war ich skeptisch. Ich hatte schon einen Ausstellungsraum und nicht das geringste Bedürfnis, einen zweiten zu betreiben. Ich mag es genauso wenig, wenn Leute mit Schuhen durch meine Wohnung laufen, wie wenn ich sie in einem Ausstellungsraum ausziehen muss. Auch habe ich die Beweggründe meines Freundes damals nicht ganz verstanden. Mir war nicht klar, wie viel Mut es erfordert, sich und seine Kunst in ein fremdes Haus einzuladen. Ich bin eine starke Verfechterin der Privatsphäre. Ich wollte nicht, dass die Leute wissen, dass ich in einer heruntergekommenen Wohnung lebe, was ich im Kühlschrank habe oder wie viele Bücher von Simone Weil ich obsessiv horte. Aber ich gab nach. Gastfreundschaft ist schliesslich das, was Kultur erst möglich macht. Am Morgen der Vernissage tauchten der Künstler und seine Frau mit einer Wagenladung unfertiger Kunstwerke auf. Während sich mir die Nackenhaare aufstellten, begannen sie, die zahlreichen Werke, die sich bereits in meinem Besitz befanden, abzuhängen und in meinem Schlafzimmer zu verstauen. Ich gab ihnen einen Vertrauensvorschuss und verliess die Wohnung, um zur Arbeit zu gehen. Wenn ich

later, while I was on a job, requesting an exhibition text. I felt
my cool crumble ever so slightly. But I obliged. I wrote about
the absurdity of inviting yourself into someone's house to
make an exhibition. I remember I threw some Louis Lavelle in
there, for good measure.

As serendipity would have it, it just so happened that I met
Hans Ulrich Obrist at work that day. He was in town harvest-
ing portfolios from young artists for his database. I don't feel
particularly obligated to do free labor for powerful curators,
but had been cajoled into meeting Obrist as a favor for—or to
keep the peace with—an acquaintance working for the host
institution. Very well. I sat through the long, droning mono-
logues, my mind firmly at home and on the potential shenani-
gans the artist might get up to in my absence, my eyes revealing that my smiles were far from heartfelt, had he bothered to
look. As we parted, Obrist asked if there were any events he
should catch during his stay. I said: Yes, there is an opening
at my house tonight. Then I scurried home in the cold, now
nervous not only about the status of the install, but acutely
aware that the artist had invited a lot of people, many of them
whom I knew to be of an energetic and lawless constitution.

110

mich recht erinnere, rief mich mein Freund später auf der
Arbeit an und bat mich um einen Ausstellungstext. Ich spürte,
wie ich langsam die Fassung verlor. Aber ich tat ihm den
Gefallen. Ich schrieb über die Absurdität, sich selbst in das
Haus von jemandem einzuladen, um eine Ausstellung zu
machen. Ich erinnere mich, dass ich eine Prise Louis Lavelle
einstreute.

Der Zufall wollte es, dass ich an diesem Tag Hans Ulrich
Obrist bei der Arbeit begegnet bin. Er war in der Stadt, um
Portfolios junger Künstler*innen für seine Onlinedatenbank
zu sammeln. Obwohl ich nicht besonders geneigt bin,
unentgeltlich für einflussreiche Kurator*innen zu arbeiten,
hatte ich mich überreden lassen, Obrist zu treffen, um einem
Bekannten, der für die gastgebende Institution arbeitete,
einen Gefallen zu tun – oder vielleicht auch, um den Frieden
mit ihm zu wahren. Wie dem auch sei. Ich liess die langen,
einschläfernden Monologe über mich ergehen, dachte an zu
Hause und an den möglichen Schabernack, den der Künstler in meiner Abwesenheit treiben könnte, und meine Augen
hätten verraten, dass mein Lächeln alles andere als
aufrichtig war, wenn er sich denn die Mühe gemacht hätte,
hinzusehen. Als wir uns verabschiedeten, fragte mich
Obrist, ob es während seines Aufenthalts noch irgendwelche
Veranstaltungen gebe, die er besuchen sollte. Ich erwähnte
die Vernissage, die am Abend bei mir stattfinden würde.
Dann eilte ich durch die Kälte nach Hause, nicht nur nervös

When I got back, several pastel and ink drawings resembling
calendars adorned my dimly lit home. People started pouring
in, soon exhausting what I had believed to be an ample supply of beer and drinks. For a moment, I feared that the floors
would give out. Someone had found the record player and
was fiddling around with the pitch controls, adding chaos
to the already cacophonous environment. I was pacing the
rooms in a failed attempt at keeping the atmosphere some-
what civilized, and avoiding being cornered by some pedants
wanting to discuss the exhibition, when my phone rang. On
the street, repeatedly pressing my defunct doorbell, stood
a certain Swiss curator with their assistant and entourage
in tow. They had heard there was an exhibition. They wanted
to see it. So up they came, their dress shoes clicking on the
stairs of my unlit five-story walk-up,and in they went. Obrist
might have taken a moment to actually look at the art, had the
apartment not been filled to the brim with people in various
stages of sonorous inebriation. One young man with a distinct
benzo glaze in his eyes attempted to sell the curator some
stolen sportswear, alarms still attached. Obrist's assistant
was trying to compliment my library when he was pushed

111

ob des Zustands der Installation, sondern auch in dem
Bewusstsein, dass der Künstler viele Menschen eingeladen
hatte, von denen ich wusste, dass sie äusserst lebhaft und
ungezügelt waren. Als ich zurückkam, schmückten mehrere
kalenderähnliche Pastell- und Tuschezeichnungen meine
spärlich beleuchtete Wohnung. Die Leute strömten herein
und leerten bald die Bier- und Getränkevorräte, die ich
für ausreichend gehalten hatte. Einen Moment lang befürch-
tete ich, der Boden würde nachgeben. Irgendjemand
hatte den Plattenspieler gefunden und spielte mit den Ton-
reglern herum, um das Chaos in der ohnehin schon ohren-
betäubenden Umgebung perfekt zu machen. Ich ging in den
Räumen auf und ab, versuchte vergeblich, die Situation
einigermassen unter Kontrolle zu halten und nicht von Besser-
wisser*innen in Beschlag genommen zu werden, die über
die Ausstellung diskutieren wollten, als mein Telefon klingelte.
Auf der Strasse stand ein gewisser Schweizer Kurator
mit seinem Assistenten und einer ganzen Entourage und
klingelte an meiner kaputten Türklingel Sturm. Sie hätten
von der Ausstellung gehört. Sie wollten sie sehen. Also
kamen sie, ihre Schuhe klapperten auf den Stufen meines
unbeleuchteten fünfstöckigen Treppenhauses, und traten
ein. Vielleicht hätte sich Obrist einen Moment Zeit genommen,
um die Kunstwerke auf sich wirken zu lassen, wäre die
Wohnung nicht bis zur Decke mit Menschen in unterschiedlichen Stadien des Delirs gefüllt gewesen. Ein junger Mann

aside by someone fleeing down the staircase to relieve him-
self—I don't know from which end. As I was standing there,
in a nearly dissociative state, Obrist approached me, thank-
ing me for the exhibition. He found it a nice reference to his
early work as a curator. Stunned, it dawned upon me that he
thought the whole event, this catastrophic desecration of my
private space, had been done in his honor. I said: Oh no, don't
thank me, I'm simply the facilitator, please meet the artist. And
that's how I got to redeem my evening by gleefully watching
my friend tense up more than I thought a human being could,
while stutteringly trying to hold a conversation with a deeply
disinterested Hans Ulrich Obrist.

112

mit einem unverkennbaren Benzoschimmer in den Augen
wollte dem Kurator gestohlene Sportkleidung andrehen,
an der noch die Alarmanlage baumelte. Obrists Assistent
liess mir gerade ein Kompliment für meine Bibliothek zuteil-
werden, als er von jemandem zur Seite gestossen wurde,
der die Treppe hinunterstürzte, um sich zu erleichtern –
ich weiss nicht, aus welcher Körperöffnung. Während ich in
einem leicht dissoziativen Zustand dastand, kam Obrist
auf mich zu und dankte mir für die Ausstellung. Er meinte,
sie sei eine schöne Referenz an sein kuratorisches Früh-
werk. Fassungslos begriff ich, dass er glaubte, die ganze
Veranstaltung, diese katastrophale Entweihung meiner
Privatsphäre, sei ihm zu Ehren geschehen. Ich erwiderte:
Oh nein, danken Sie nicht mir, ich bin nur die Gastgeberin,
darf ich vorstellen, der Künstler. Und so bin ich an diesem
Abend doch noch auf meine Kosten gekommen, indem
ich genüsslich beobachtete, wie mein Freund sich mehr
verkrampfte als ich es für menschenmöglich gehalten
hätte, während er stotternd versuchte, ein Gespräch mit
einem zutiefst desinteressierten Hans Ulrich Obrist zu
führen.

Hospitality is what makes culture possible

I remember moving cities as a young art student, wincing at my memories of feeble attempts at navigating a new place, a new scene, and new social circles. My new school was entirely different to my undergrad academy: in comparison, it was rigid, bureaucratic, labyrinthian, and forbidding. There was a chain of command that wasn't expressly taught, but only became clear once you were reprimanded for breaking it. The building was like a vault. Should a newcomer happen to slip through the wrong door while it was propped open, they were at risk of being trapped in there, unless they had access to the lock, programmed into the key cards the smuggest students wore like jewelry or a badge of honor at all times and in any setting. My new classmates quickly started behaving like weeds, shooting up and sprouting through the cracks of the reinforced concrete, attempting to thrive, to make the property more accommodating on a human scale. A potted plant here. A rug there. Suspiciously stained sofas hauled from God knows where during the night, after the disapproving eyes of the staff had retired for the evening. Communal dinners in

113

Gastfreundschaft macht Kultur erst möglich

Noch heute schaudert es mich, wenn ich daran denke, wie ich als junge Kunststudentin versuchte, mich in einer neuen Stadt, einer neuen Umgebung und in neuen sozialen Kreisen zurechtzufinden. Meine neue Schule war ganz anders als die, an der ich meinen Bachelor gemacht hatte: Sie war im Vergleich starr, bürokratisch, labyrinthisch und abweisend. Es gab eine Befehlskette, die nicht explizit kommuniziert wurde, die man aber zu spüren bekam, wenn man wegen eines Verstosses gegen sie gerügt wurde. Das Gebäude glich einem Hochsicherheitsgefängnis: Schlüpfte ein Neuankömmling durch die falsche offene Tür, lief er Gefahr, in dem Raum gefangen zu sein, es sei denn, er hatte Zugang zu einer der digitalen Schlüsselkarten, die die Hochnäsigsten unter den Studierenden wie Schmuck oder Ehrenabzeichen ständig und überall bei sich trugen. Meine neuen Kommiliton*innen begannen schnell, sich wie Unkraut zu benehmen, wuchsen in die Höhe, drängten sich durch die Risse im Stahlbeton, versuchten zu gedeihen, den Ort menschlicher zu gestalten. Eine Topfpflanze hier. Ein Teppich dort. Verdächtig fleckige Sofas, die nachts von Gott weiss woher herbeigeschafft wurden, nachdem sich die missbilligenden Blicke des Personals für den Abend zurückgezogen hatten. Gemeinsame Abendessen im verliesartigen Keller, der uns als „Sozialraum" zugewiesen

the dungeon-like basement we were allotted as our "social space," before the secret and highly prohibited installment of illegal hot plates in the more habitable areas of the building, rented from private property sharks for eye-watering annual sums. We banded together and sought small ways to carve out a space for learning, mostly from one another.

The artist-run spaces in this new city, ever alluring, seemed like underground societies to me in the early days. As if I needed to know a secret knock to enter. I would never have admitted it to anyone, least of all myself, but visiting these spaces made me uneasy. Always taking care to mask my nervousness—or so I hoped—behind tightly sealed lips and a deadpan expression, I continued going to the openings. The stiff ones with blaring fluorescent light, imitating the blue-chip circuit I doubt many of them had seen much of apart from in digital images; the hidden ones in decrepit squats behind steel doors and dark courtyards; the semi-private ones where shoes had to be removed and drinks were taken from refriger-ators holding the inhabitant's cheese and topical antibiotics. I went to the rowdy ones where the guests were 95 percent (intoxicated) men, exhibiting work by 95 percent (intoxicated)

wurde, bevor die heimliche und streng verbotene Installation illegaler Kochplatten in den bewohnbareren Teilen des Gebäudes erfolgte, die von privaten Immobilienhaien für horrende jährliche Summen angemietet wurden. Wir taten uns zusammen und suchten nach kleinen Möglichkeiten, einen Raum zu schaffen, um zu lernen – vor allem voneinander.

Die Offspaces in dieser neuen, aufregenden Stadt kamen mir anfangs wie Geheimbünde vor. Als müsste ich ein geheimes Klopfzeichen kennen, um eintreten zu können. Ich hätte es mir damals nie eingestanden, aber der Besuch dieser Räume verunsicherte mich. Ich musste stets darauf achten, meine Nervosität hinter fest geschlossenen Lippen und einem ausdruckslosen Gesicht zu verbergen, was mir nicht immer gelang. Die spiessigen mit grellem Neon-licht, die eine Kunstwelt imitierten, die viele von ihnen wahrscheinlich nur von digitalen Bildern kannten; die in her-untergekommenen besetzten Häusern hinter Stahltüren und in dunklen Hinterhöfen versteckten; die halbprivaten, wo man die Schuhe ausziehen musste und die Getränke aus Kühlschränken kamen, in denen der Käse und die Anti-biotika der Bewohner*innen lagerten. Ich ging zu den Lauten, wo die Gäste zu 95 Prozent aus (betrunkenen) Männer bestanden, die zu 95 Prozent (betrunkene) Männer ausstell-ten. Die anfängliche Einschüchterung wich schnell einem Gefühl der – mir will kein besserer Ausdruck einfallen – Dankbarkeit. Dankbarkeit dafür, dass der Besuch und sogar

men. Rapidly, the intimidation I had initially experienced gave way to a feeling of—for want of a better expression—gratitude. Gratitude at discovering that visiting and even running an exhibition space was not some inherited right granted only to a few, chosen people. A capacity for work, collaboration, and being sociable seemed enough. Or was that youthful hubris?

Immediately after graduation, I had the privilege of testing my suspicion that it was in fact possible to simply start an artist-run space. Three dear colleagues and I decided that if we wanted fun things to happen, we might as well *make* them happen. The first location for the space, which we proudly kept afloat for five years, was in a dingy, underground, former superintendent's apartment in a picturesque and wealthy part of town. It was freezing cold, even in summer. To use the toilet or access the fuse box (both common necessities, the latter often more frequently), we had to pass through a basement and the courtyard. We became amateur electricians, plumbers, bartenders, caterers, we learned how to repair monitors and how to code in Linux. Occasionally, we were therapists. Frequently, tour guides. We were baffled at how

115

die Leitung eines Ausstellungsraums kein ererbtes Recht ist, das nur wenigen Auserwählten gewährt wird. Die Fähigkeit zu arbeiten, zusammenzuarbeiten und gesellig zu sein schien zu genügen. Oder entsprang diese Annahme jugendlicher Hybris?

Unmittelbar nach meinem Abschluss hatte ich die Gelegenheit, meine Vermutung zu überprüfen, dass es ohne weiteres möglich ist, einen selbstorganisierten Ausstellungsraum zu eröffnen. Drei liebe Kolleg*innen und ich kamen zu dem Schluss, dass wenn etwas Aufregendes passieren sollte, dann müssten wir die Sache selbst in die Hand nehmen. Der erste Standort des Ausstellungsraums, der sich fünf Jahre lang über Wasser hielt, war eine schäbige Kellerwohnung eines ehemaligen Hausmeisters in einem malerischen Villenviertel. Dort war es selbst im Sommer eiskalt. Um auf die Toilette zu gehen oder an den Sicherungskasten zu gelangen (beides alltägliche Notwendigkeiten, wobei das Letztere öfter vorkam), mussten wir durch den Keller und über den Hof gehen. Wir wurden zu Hobbyelektrikerinnen, Klempnerinnen, Barkeeperinnen, Caterinnen, lernten, Monitore zu reparieren und in Linux zu programmieren. Manchmal waren wir Therapeutinnen. Oft waren wir Reiseleiterinnen. Wir waren verblüfft, wie bereitwillig die angefragten Künstler*innen unsere Einladungen annahmen, in einem neuen, dürftigen und brüchigen Raum auszustellen, weit weg von den Galerie-Hotspots der

eagerly artists accepted our invitations to exhibit in a new, impoverished, and wonky space, far from the gallery hotspots of the city. As far as I remember, nobody ever said no, not even during the early days when we paid for everything ourselves and loaned equipment from the other spaces around town, transporting it on our bicycles. Perhaps it was the novelty, perhaps it was pity, perhaps it was the earnestness with which we presented our project, or perhaps it was the pizza parties and our commitment to stand by the artists every step of the way from idea to opening. Perhaps it was beginner's luck.

I spent more time in that frigid basement than in my own home. I think we all did. We tended to the space with the utmost care, with a hobby gardener's pride. One of us worked as a florist on the side, and we were often delighted by the addition of huge, baroque bouquets, comically luxurious and a stark contrast to our space, held together by sheer tyranny of will, pro bono work, and ever-increasing layers of plaster. But of course, the project was not about us. Our aim was to help artists to realize their projects, however vague, ambitious, and improbable they might have been. The exhibition space, we believed, should be a nesting ground for mostly young

Stadt. Soweit ich mich erinnere, hat noch nie jemand abgelehnt, nicht einmal in den ersten Tagen, als wir alles selbst bezahlten und das Equipment von anderen Ausstellungsräumen in der Stadt ausliehen und auf unseren Fahrrädern transportierten. Vielleicht lag es an dem Neuheitsfaktor, vielleicht am Mitleid, vielleicht an der Ernsthaftigkeit, mit der wir unser Projekt vorstellten, vielleicht an den Pizza-Partys und unserem Engagement, den Künstler*innen bei jedem Schritt von der Idee bis zur Eröffnung zur Seite zu stehen. Vielleicht war es auch Anfängerglück.

Ich habe mehr Zeit in diesem kalten Keller verbracht als in meinem eigenen Zuhause. Ich glaube, so ging es uns allen. Wir pflegten den Raum mit grosser Sorgfalt und dem Stolz von Hobbygärtnerinnen. Eine von uns arbeitete nebenbei als Floristin, und wir freuten uns oft über die riesigen barocken Blumensträusse, deren skurriler Luxus in krassem Gegensatz zu unserem Raum stand, der nur durch reine Willenskraft, freiwillige Arbeit und immer neue Putzschichten zusammengehalten wurde. Aber natürlich ging es bei dem Projekt nicht um uns. Unser Ziel war es, die Künstler*innen bei der Verwirklichung ihrer Projekte zu unterstützen, wie vage, ehrgeizig und unwahrscheinlich ihre Vorhaben auch sein mochten. Unserer Überzeugung nach sollte der Ausstellungsraum ein Nährboden für vor allem junge Künstler*innen sein, ein Ort, an dem sie ihre

artists, a place to realize their solo exhibitions outside of the institutional framework that, at least in my experience, has a tendency to slowly, slowly, in a process that could be likened to editing, mold any project to fit their profile. As a result, we showed all kinds of practices. Some affirmative of the current trends, of course. Many idiosyncratic and delightfully absurd. During one particular production meeting, the exhibiting artist explained that they wanted to make a show about "everything," but struggled to find the words to describe what they meant. I suggested it might be easier to sketch the idea on a piece of paper. The artist sat in palpable concentration for a while, before revealing the drawing: a singular, horizontal line across the paper. I was speechless. My colleague said: Ok, let's do it. It became a strange, endearing exhibition with impressive scope, put together with admirable nonchalance and elegance.

Running an exhibition space in this way takes a lot of trust, from both the artists and the curators.

The pleasure of making exhibitions, usually one a month, was so great that it justified the workload. It had all of the excitement of exhibiting your own work, but only about half

Einzelausstellungen ausserhalb des institutionellen Rahmens realisieren können, der zumindest meiner Erfahrung nach dazu neigt, jedes Projekt in einem Prozess, den man mit dem eines Lektorats vergleichen könnte, fast unmerklich so zu formen, dass es in sein Profil passt. Wir haben also alle möglichen künstlerischen Praktiken gezeigt. Natürlich auch solche, die den aktuellen Trends entsprachen. Vieles war originell und herrlich absurd. Bei einem Treffen zur Vorbereitung der Ausstellung erklärte der ausstellende Künstler, dass er eine Ausstellung über „alles" machen wolle, aber Schwierigkeiten habe, die richtigen Worte zu finden, um zu erklären, was er meine. Ich schlug vor, die Idee auf einem Blatt Papier zu skizzieren. Der Künstler sass eine Weile in spürbarer Konzentration da, bevor er die Zeichnung enthüllte: eine einzige horizontale Linie quer über das Papier. Ich war sprachlos. Meine Kollegin meinte: Okay, machen wir das. Es wurde eine seltsame, liebenswerte Ausstellung mit einer beeindruckenden Bandbreite an Themen, die mit bewundernswerter Lässigkeit und Eleganz zusammengestellt wurde. Einen Ausstellungsraum auf diese Weise zu führen, erfordert viel Vertrauen, sowohl vonseiten der Künstler*innen als auch der Galerist*innen.

Die Freude am Ausstellungsmachen, in der Regel eine pro Monat, war so gross, dass sie den Arbeitsaufwand aufwog. Es war genauso aufregend wie das Ausstellen eigener Arbeiten, aber nur halb so beängstigend. Zumindest im

the angst. In hindsight at least, it was one of the most reward-
ing and educational periods of my life. I didn't question never
having weekends off, running to the space to tend to yet
another thing that was now in disrepair, or hauling miter saws
across the city on foot. We didn't get frustrated when an artist wasn't finished installing their work until after the show
had opened. We sifted through disjointed notes for gold. We
dressed up for the occasion. The four of us organizing the
space developed a peculiar type of choreography. When the
workflow worked, it was intoxicating, incomparable. Becoming a unit of very different individuals, coming together for a
shared cause, and seeing that it worked, that it had become
what we had hoped it could become, was really something.
Many artists we held in high esteem benefited, and we benefited, too. It was a malleable project, shaped by everyone
who honored us with their exhibitions, their trust, and their
work. It taught me how to hit the ground running, how to sol-
der, how to program party lights, and how to console terrified
artists. It taught me how to properly use Excel spreadsheets,
and which boutiques to go to when you desperately need to
borrow a steamer for just thirty minutes. It taught me how to

Nachhinein war es eine der lohnendsten und lehrreichsten
Phasen meines Lebens. Es war mir egal, dass ich kein
freies Wochenende hatte, dass ich dauernd in den Ausstellungsraum rennen musste, um noch etwas zu reparieren,
oder dass ich Gehrungssägen zu Fuss durch die Stadt
schleppen musste. Es machte uns nichts aus, wenn ein*e
Künstler*in ihr Werk erst nach der Eröffnung der Ausstellung fertig installierte. Wir schürften in zusammenhang-
losen Notizen nach Gold. Wir machten uns für die Ver-
nissagen schick. Wir vier, die den Raum organisierten,
entwickelten unsere eigene Choreografie. Wenn alles
klappte, war es berauschend – ein unvergleichliches Gefühl.
Aus völlig unterschiedlichen Individuen wurde eine Einheit,
die sich für eine gemeinsame Sache zusammenfand.
Zu sehen, dass es funktionierte, dass es das wurde, was wir
uns erhofft hatten, war wirklich sehr besonders. Viele
Künstler*innen, die wir schätzten, haben davon profitiert,
und wir auch. Es war ein formbares Projekt, das von all
denen geprägt wurde, die uns mit ihren Ausstellungen, ihrem
Vertrauen und ihrer Arbeit geehrt haben. Ich lernte, wie
man sofort loslegt, wie man lötet, wie man Partylichter
programmiert und wie man verängstigte Künstler*innen
tröstet. Ich lernte, wie man mit Excel-Tabellen umgeht
und wo man sich ein Dampfbügeleisen für 30 Minuten aus-
leihen kann, wenn man es dringend braucht. Ich lernte,
wirklich zusammenzuarbeiten und die Kontrolle abzugeben,

truly collaborate, to surrender the control I've so desperately sought throughout my life. But mostly, it taught me about hospitality.

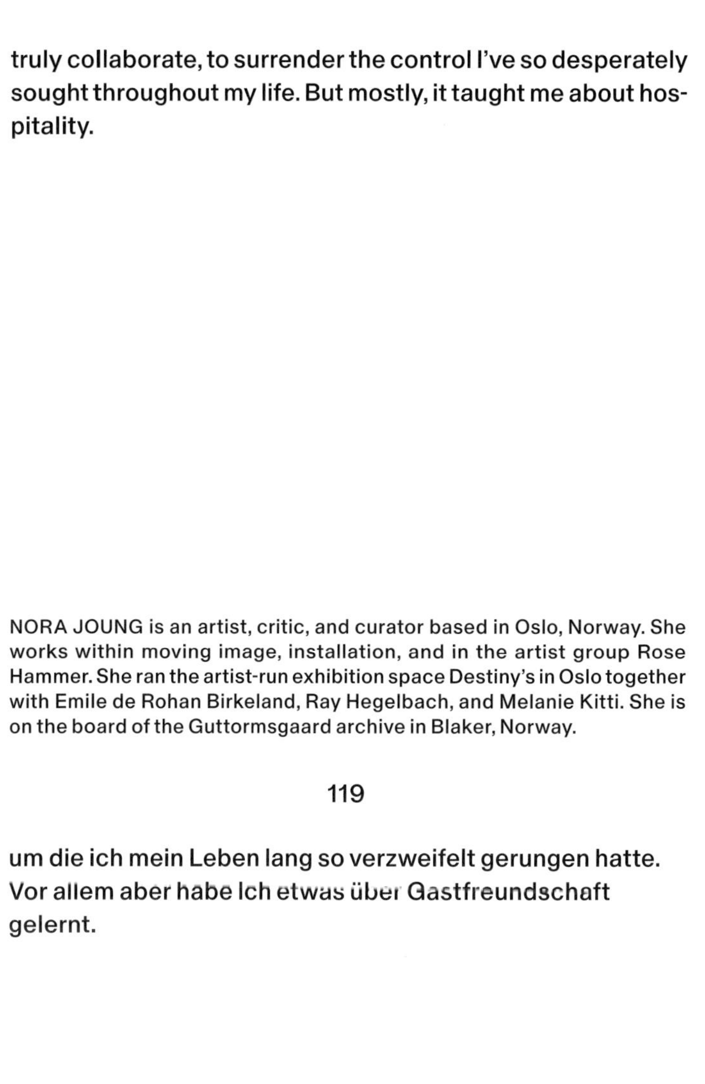

NORA JOUNG is an artist, critic, and curator based in Oslo, Norway. She works within moving image, installation, and in the artist group Rose Hammer. She ran the artist-run exhibition space Destiny's in Oslo together with Emile de Rohan Birkeland, Ray Hegelbach, and Melanie Kitti. She is on the board of the Guttormsgaard archive in Blaker, Norway.

um die ich mein Leben lang so verzweifelt gerungen hatte. Vor allem aber habe Ich etwas über Gastfreundschaft gelernt.

NORA JOUNG ist eine Künstlerin, Kritikerin und Kuratorin und lebt in Oslo, Norwegen. Sie arbeitet in den Bereichen Bewegtbild und Installation sowie in der Künstler*innengruppe Rose Hammer. Zusammen mit Emile de Rohan Birkeland, Ray Hegelbach und Melanie Kitti leitete sie den von Künstler*innen geführten Ausstellungsraum Destiny's in Oslo. Sie ist Vorstandsmitglied des Guttormsgaard-Archivs in Blaker, Norwegen.

In conversation with Palazzina

Im Gespräch mit Palazzina

Marlene Marti Bürgi & Kelly Tissot, Ines Tondar, Nicolás Sarmiento, Noemi Pfister, Simone Holliger, Vera Mühlebach, Victoria Holdt

It's July, pretty humid. It might start to rain at some point. But we'll take our chances, because the green, overgrown backyard is slightly cooler than the rest of Allschwil. We're sitting around a few tables with lots of beautiful food. The art of hosting is as much a part of Palazzina as living and exhibition-making. At the moment, ten people are sharing the house at Baslerstrasse 321. Artists, curators, architects. As an association, however, a total of thirteen people contribute to the offspace, an artist-run space that started in 2019. It's a democratic structure that brings together a multitude of voices interested in being together, having conversations, and realizing projects that go far beyond the house itself.

It's with these voices that I get to talk about questions of space—having space, taking space, sharing space, collective space, needing (more or less) space, systemic space. Beyond the sociopolitical issues that these aspects raise, Palazzina has to negotiate some of these spaces on a daily basis. On that note, let's talk and eat.

121

Ein schwüler Tag im Juli. Jeden Moment könnte es anfangen zu regnen. Aber wir riskieren es, denn der begrünte Hinterhof ist etwas kühler als der Rest von Allschwil. Wir sitzen an Tischen, die mit wunderbarem Essen gedeckt sind. Die Kunst des Gastgebens gehört zu Palazzina wie das gemeinschaftliche Wohnen und das Ausstellungsmachen. Derzeit leben zehn Personen im Haus in der Baslerstrasse 321: Künstler*innen, Kurator*innen, Architekt*innen. Der Verein, der hinter dem 2019 ins Leben gerufenen Offspace steht, zählt inzwischen dreizehn Mitglieder. Diese demokratische Organisation vereint viele verschiedenen Stimmen, die sich für das Zusammensein, den Austausch und die Realisierung von Projekten interessieren, die weit über das Haus als solches hinausgehen.

Mit diesen Stimmen darf ich über Raumfragen sprechen – Raum haben, Raum einnehmen, Raum teilen, gemeinschaftlicher Raum, (mehr oder weniger) Raum brauchen, systemischer Raum. Abgesehen von der gesellschaftspolitischen Dimension, die diese Aspekte aufwerfen, muss das Kollektiv Palazzina über einige dieser Räume täglich verhandeln. In diesem Sinne: Lasst uns diskutieren und essen!

MARLENE Looking at Palazzina, I'm curious to hear about the house and your collective structure, since you share both personal and professional spaces with each other. What is your understanding of a collective at this point? What is the rhythm that you've developed in these two different spaces like?

NICOLÁS Actually, there's a flux of members coming and going, sometimes renting rooms temporarily. The house itself is an administration that isn't necessarily related to the exhibition projects. When we meet for the offspace, we don't really talk about the house—it's just there. Living together doesn't always involve talking about work; it's like being with a friend where work isn't the focus. The experience changes over time as new members join. Those who've been here longer might have different stories about the past when everything was much more chaotic and intense. NOEMI Still, 90 percent of the people that are part of the collective live here, so it's not totally disconnected. KELLY It's a little weird to think about "the house" because we've had so many houses. It's more like an entity we navigate around. I don't live here anymore, but

MARLENE Mit Blick auf Palazzina würde ich gerne mehr über das Haus und eure Struktur als Kollektiv erfahren, da ihr sowohl private als auch berufliche Räume miteinander teilt. Was versteht ihr unter einem Kollektiv? Welchen Rhythmus habt ihr in diesen beiden unterschiedlichen Räumen entwickelt?

NICOLÁS Die Mitglieder wechseln häufig, da einige nur vorübergehend ein Zimmer mieten. Die Administration des Hauses selbst hängt nicht unbedingt mit den Ausstellungsprojekten zusammen. Wenn wir uns wegen des Offspaces treffen, reden wir nicht wirklich über das Haus – es ist einfach da. Beim Zusammenleben geht es nicht immer um die Arbeit, es ist wie mit Freund*innen, bei denen die Arbeit nicht im Vordergrund steht. Die Erfahrung ändert sich mit der Zeit, wenn neue Mitglieder hinzukommen. Diejenigen, die schon länger dabei sind, können sich vielleicht an eine Zeit erinnern, als alles noch viel chaotischer und unsteter war. NOEMI Dennoch leben hier 90 Prozent der Menschen, die Teil des Kollektivs sind. Das Haus und der Offspace sind also nicht vollständig voneinander abgekoppelt. KELLY Es klingt in meinen Ohren ein bisschen komisch, vom „Haus" zu sprechen, weil es so viele Häuser gab. Es ist eher eine Art Entität, um die wir uns drehen. Ich wohne nicht mehr hier, aber das Haus ist immer noch irgendwie präsent, egal in welchem Haus

the house still has a presence somehow, whichever house or space it is—it's more like an idea in a way. I like that it's quite comfortable and warm. It's like an imaginary roof that makes it different from other offspaces. We could be somewhere else next year, and it would still feel like Palazzina.

> MARLENE Indeed, Palazzina has this comforting presence beyond a physical space and a geographical location. Looking back at the history of Palazzina, in what sense has your concept of the collective evolved from your first exhibition until now?

VICTORIA In a way, the space feels like an organism. We planted a seed at our first house on Schweizergasse, and each member who joined contributed to Palazzina, making it different with each new place we moved to. I feel it is still similar in a way—always changing, of course. Not only because of the people, but also each new place we've been to. NOEMI We started in a really genuine way. Vicki and I had finished our master's degrees and were a bit lost after our studies, living in a new city. Then there was this opportunity of an empty

123

oder an welchem Ort Palazzina gerade angesiedelt ist – es ist eher eine Idee als ein physischer Ort. Mir gefällt, dass die Idee so ziemlich gemütlich und warm ist. Es ist wie ein imaginäres Dach, was Palazzina von anderen Offspaces unterscheidet. Nächstes Jahr könnten wir in einem anderen Haus sitzen und es würde sich immer noch wie Palazzina anfühlen.

> MARLENE Palazzina hat tatsächlich eine behagliche Präsenz, die über einen physischen Raum und einen geografischen Ort hinausgeht. Wie hat sich eure Vorstellung vom Kollektiv seit eurer ersten Ausstellung im Palazzina bis heute entwickelt?

VICTORIA In gewisser Weise fühlt sich der Raum wie ein Organismus an. Wir haben in unserem ersten Haus in der Schweizergasse einen Samen gepflanzt, und jedes Mitglied, das zu uns gestossen ist, hat etwas zu Palazzina beigetragen und an jedem neuen Standort mitgestaltet. Ich habe das Gefühl, dass Palazzina sich treu geblieben ist. Trotzdem ist es natürlich in ständigem Wandel – nicht nur wegen der unterschiedlichen Menschen, sondern auch wegen jedem neuen Standort. NOEMI Unsere Anfänge waren sehr bescheiden. Vicki und ich hatten gerade unseren Master abgeschlossen und waren etwas orientierungslos, weil wir in einer neuen Stadt lebten. Dann bekamen wir

house, which looked super cool. We thought that it could be an exhibition space, and we could find other roommates who were interested in the same thing. In the beginning, we were just trying to figure it all out: What should we do? Who could we invite?   VICTORIA   We started growing. When we encountered challenges, we knew how to tackle them better the next time.

MARLENE   The idea of growth—of both people and knowledge—is great, but it still ties back to a figurative house that embodies the organism or entity. When I think of Palazzina, I think about a housing structure. Even *Palazzina On Foot*[1] has a pavilion structure—you even have a roof over it. Are you also growing the organism, the house and the spaces? How has this growth manifested in terms of the professionalism and organization of the offspace?

KELLY   For me, Palazzina has grown in different ways. It's not just the project that has grown; we have grown as artists, too. After five years, we are all in a different place than when we

124

die Gelegenheit, in ein leerstehendes Haus zu ziehen, das supercool aussah. Wir dachten, dass es ein Ausstellungsraum sein könnte und wir andere Mitbewohner*innen finden könnten, die unser Interesse teilten. Zuerst versuchten wir einfach, uns einen Überblick zu verschaffen: Was sollen wir machen? Wen könnten wir einladen?   VICTORIA   Wir sind an den Herausforderungen gewachsen und haben gelernt, sie immer besser zu meistern.

MARLENE   Die Idee des Wachstums – sowohl von Menschen als auch von Wissen – ist grossartig, aber sie ist immer mit einem buchstäblichen Haus verbunden, das den Organismus oder eine Entität verkörpert. Wenn ich an Palazzina denke, denke ich an ein Haus. Sogar *Palazzina On Foot*[1] hat eine Pavillonstruktur – mit einem Dach darüber. Lasst ihr auch den Organismus, das Haus, die Räume wachsen? Wie manifestiert sich dieses Wachstum hinsichtlich der Professionalität und Organisation des Offspaces?

KELLY   Für mich ist Palazzina in vielerlei Hinsicht gewachsen. Nicht nur das Projekt ist gewachsen, sondern auch wir als Künstler*innen. Nach fünf Jahren sind wir alle an einem anderen Punkt als am Anfang. Wir kommen jetzt mit neuen Publikumsgruppen und neuen Künstler*innengenerationen in Kontakt, aber wir sind immer noch da und

started. Now we're also engaging with new crowds and new generations of artists, but we're still here and getting older. It's a nice way to see the scene evolve while staying connected. We also have new members. In the beginning there were six of us, and now this has more than doubled.   INES   The growth has been quite organic, actually. We didn't have a specific goal that we needed to reach. We just had the wish to join forces and create something together. We expanded our knowledge and members very naturally with each new house and encounter.   NOEMI   From the beginning, hosting has been central, like now, when we're having an apéro. This is a typical Palazzina moment. When we invite artists for projects, we offer them food and a place to sleep. When we host artists, we have an exchange, we can learn from them, too. It's more than just networking, which sounds so stupid; it's about creating connections . . .   VICTORIA   . . . creating exchanges and encounters in order to share moments together like this as well.   NOEMI   It also sharpens our personal practices, because you see things, you discuss things, you try to figure things out.   VERA   Regarding the professional side of growth, I wanted to add that as a late member of Palazzina,

125

werden älter. Es ist schön zu sehen, wie sich die Szene entwickelt, während man in Kontakt bleibt. Wir haben auch neue Mitglieder. Am Anfang waren wir zu sechst, jetzt sind wir mehr als doppelt so viele.   INES   Das Wachstum hat sich eigentlich ganz organisch ergeben. Wir hatten kein bestimmtes Ziel, das wir erreichen mussten. Wir hatten einfach den Wunsch, unsere Kräfte zu bündeln und gemeinsam etwas zu schaffen. Mit jedem neuen Haus und jeder neuen Begegnung haben wir unser Wissen und unsere Mitgliederzahl organisch erweitert.   NOEMI   Von Anfang an stand die Gastfreundschaft im Mittelpunkt, so wie jetzt beim Apéro – ein typischer Palazzina-Moment. Wenn wir Künstler*innen für Projekte einladen, bieten wir ihnen Verpflegung und einen Schlafplatz an. Wenn wir Künstler*innen bei uns aufnehmen, findet ein Austausch statt und wir können von ihnen lernen. Es geht um mehr als Networking, was blöd klingt, es geht darum, Verbindungen zu schaffen …   VICTORIA   … Austausch und Begegnungen schaffen, um auch solche Momente miteinander teilen zu können.   NOEMI   Es schärft auch unsere jeweilige persönliche Praxis, weil man Dinge sieht, über Dinge diskutiert und versucht, Dinge zu verstehen.   VERA   Was das berufliche Wachstum betrifft, möchte ich hinzufügen, dass ich als spätes Mitglied von Palazzina festgestellt habe, wie stabil und doch nicht hierarchisch die Struktur ist. Sie ist zugleich professionell und kollektiv und ähnelt

I've noticed how stable yet non-hierarchical the structure is. It's professional but collective, much more like shared living. You take care of the members in the house and you get taken care of too, you try to engage, you try to find moments for exchange. In that sense, it's very different from a typical professional environment.

MARLENE   There are many different voices coming together at Palazzina, different people, different minds, different languages. So, you have to find ways to communicate and work together. How do you find a common language or way of collaborating with so many different minds and perspectives?

VERA   Trust is very important in this kind of collaborative work. You have to trust others, to feel comfortable with sharing what you think, to support anything the others want to propose or do. Flexibility and openness are also key, since things evolve organically and you can't control everything anyway.   INES   We have lots of meetings where we share ideas and tasks. We respect and always learn from each other

126

daher dem Leben in einer Wohngemeinschaft. Wir kümmern uns um die Mitglieder des Haushalts und wir kümmern uns um uns selbst, wir versuchen, uns zu engagieren, wir versuchen, Momente des Austauschs zu finden. In dieser Hinsicht unterscheidet sich die Struktur sehr von einer typischen Arbeitsumgebung.

MARLENE   Im Palazzina kommen viele verschiedene Stimmen zusammen, verschiedene Menschen, verschiedene Denkweisen, verschiedene Sprachen. Ihr müsst also Wege finden, um zu kommunizieren und zusammenzuarbeiten. Wie findet ihr eine gemeinsame Sprache oder einen Modus der Zusammenarbeit mit so vielen verschiedenen Denkweisen und Perspektiven?

VERA   Vertrauen ist bei dieser Art der Zusammenarbeit sehr wichtig. Wir müssen den anderen vertrauen, uns wohl damit fühlen, die eigene Meinung zu teilen, und die anderen in ihren Vorhaben unterstützen. Auch Flexibilität und Offenheit sind entscheidend, da sich die Dinge organisch entwickeln und wir sowieso nicht alles unter Kontrolle haben können.   INES   Wir treffen uns regelmässig, um Ideen auszutauschen und Aufgaben zu verteilen. Wir respektieren uns gegenseitig und lernen immer wieder voneinander, wenn Ausstellungen anstehen. Ich glaube,

when exhibitions are approaching. I think Nico once said in an interview that the power we have is because there are so many of us. I think this also gives us a certain flexibility and allows us to step back when needed, or to take some time to gain energy for new projects, knowing that others will step in if they need to.　SIMONE　It has actually become more complex over time, with more layers and more projects. There is a different mode of working now, because there's more pressure. Working together now requires more coordination, communication on different channels, and more commitment, but it's also more professional. Compared to the beginning, the relationship with the house has changed, because for the first time it's not a temporary setting. Before, I saw the house much more as a tool that gave us a lot of freedom to create, to invent, to do whatever we wanted. Now, we have to take care of the house. We have to test the limits and see where we can push them, see how we can invent and reinvent the given structures, which are less flexible than the previous ones. Maybe this is also the reason why *On Foot* was born, as a way of creating a new and adaptable space outside.

127

Nico hat einmal in einem Interview gesagt, dass unsere Stärke darin liegt, dass wir so viele sind. Ich denke, das gibt uns auch eine gewisse Flexibilität und die Möglichkeit, uns zurückzuziehen oder uns eine Auszeit zu nehmen, um Energie für neue Projekte zu sammeln, in dem Wissen, dass die anderen einspringen, falls nötig.　SIMONE　Im Laufe der Zeit ist Palazzina tatsächlich komplexer geworden, mit mehr Ebenen und mehr Projekten. Die Arbeitsweise hat sich verändert, weil der Druck grösser geworden ist. Die Zusammenarbeit erfordert jetzt mehr Koordination, Kommunikation über verschiedene Kanäle und mehr Engagement, aber sie ist auch professioneller geworden. Im Vergleich zu den Anfängen hat sich die Beziehung zum Haus verändert, weil es zum ersten Mal kein temporäres Setting ist. Früher habe ich das Haus viel mehr als ein Mittel gesehen, das uns viel Freiheit gab, zu gestalten, zu erfinden, zu tun, was immer wir wollten. Jetzt müssen wir uns um das Haus kümmern. Wir müssen die Grenzen austesten und sehen, wo wir sie verschieben können, wie wir die vorgegebenen Strukturen, die weniger flexibel sind als früher, erfinden und neu erfinden können. Vielleicht wurde *On Foot* auch deshalb ins Leben gerufen, um einen neuen und anpassungsfähigen Raum im Aussen zu schaffen.

MARLENE　Die Frage nach Einschränkungen ist interessant, vor allem weil sie ziemlich widersprüchlich ist:

MARLENE   The question of limitations is interesting, particularly because it's quite contradictory: the previous houses were always temporary, which resulted in more freedom. Now, without this time restriction, you have other limitations that you have to deal with. How do you navigate the limits of space, resources, and time? What are some limits that need to be stretched?

VICTORIA   Previously, when we only had a year and a half or maybe two years per house, each artist could choose a different place in the house. After a cycle of almost two years at Baslerstrasse, we've used almost every corner. It's a little bit like, "Oh, we've seen this before." So it's a challenge to come up with ideas that are not redundant and limiting in that sense.   NOEMI   As a result, we saw a lot of potential in empty spaces outside the house. We started to fantasize a little about whether we could have a show in the shop next door. This is also a political issue, especially when we see a lot of empty places in general that don't want to host cultural projects because of other economic reasons.   NICOLÁS   Other spaces like galleries, offspaces, and museums face similar

128

Die bisherigen Häuser waren immer temporär, was euch ein grösseres Mass an Freiheit ermöglicht hat. Jetzt, ohne diese zeitliche Begrenzung, gibt es andere Einschränkungen, mit denen ihr umgehen müsst. Wie geht ihr mit den Grenzen von Raum, Ressourcen und Zeit um? Welche Grenzen müssen verschoben oder überwunden werden?

VICTORIA   Früher, als wir nur anderthalb oder vielleicht zwei Jahre pro Haus hatten, konnten alle Künstler*innen einen Ort im Haus wählen. Nach fast zwei Jahren in der Baslerstrasse haben wir fast jede Ecke genutzt. Es ist ein bisschen wie: „Oh, das haben wir schon mal gesehen." Es ist also eine Herausforderung, Ideen zu entwickeln, die nicht redundant und in diesem Sinne einschränkend sind.   NOEMI   Deshalb hatten die ungenutzten Räume ausserhalb des Hauses in unseren Augen ein grosses Potenzial. Wir fingen an, darüber nachzudenken, ob wir nicht im Laden nebenan eine Ausstellung machen könnten. Das ist auch ein politisches Anliegen, denn generell gibt es viele ungenutzte Orte, die aus anderen wirtschaftlichen Gründen nicht für Kulturprojekte genutzt werden dürfen. NICOLÁS   Galerien, Offspaces und Museen haben ähnliche räumliche Beschränkungen. Jeder Ausstellungsraum enthält im Grunde alle vorherigen Ausstellungen. Wir müssen alle innerhalb der Grenzen unserer Räume arbeiten,

spatial limitations. Every exhibition space actually contains
all the shows that went before, too. We all have to work within
the constraints of our spaces, but it forces us to think cre-
atively about new formats and approaches. When new artists
come in, there's always the possibility that they'll think and
engage differently with the space than anyone who's come
before. But sometimes they want the space to be more like
a white cube, and there are only a few artists who are really
doing strange things. For example, San Keller's work at
Alemannengasse, which included our house key.[2] Even if we
would sometimes like to see more site-specific projects, as
organizers we don't create the work and aren't in a position
to push for it. Before we moved, our formats and ideas were
simple and open, we didn't have titles for the shows. Now
we are thinking about more specific formats for the house.
NOEMI   There are other exceptions, like Vicente Lesser
Gutierrez, who discovered things about our house that even
we didn't know. It was super nice to have him here: he sneaked
around and checked where the pipes were connected in the
house. He discovered that the house apparently used to have
a chimney, and he put a sound installation in this old chimney

aber das zwingt uns dazu, kreativ über neue Formate und
Herangehensweisen nachzudenken. Wenn neue Künstler*innen dazukommen, besteht immer die Möglichkeit, dass
sie anders denken und sich auf andere Weise mit dem
Raum auseinandersetzen als alle, die vorher da waren. Manchmal wünschen sie sich aber auch, dass die Räume mehr
einem White Cube ähneln, und es gibt nur wenige Künstler*innen, die wirklich schräge Projekte umsetzen. Zum
Beispiel die Arbeit von San Keller in der Alemannengasse,
die unseren Hausschlüssel beinhaltete.[2] Auch wenn wir
uns manchmal stärker ortsspezifische Projekte wünschen,
sind wir als Organisator*innen nicht die Urheber*innen
der Werke und können darauf nicht drängen. Vor dem Umzug
waren unsere Formate und Ideen einfach und offen, die
Ausstellungen hatten keine Titel. Jetzt denken wir über
spezifische Formate für das Haus nach.   NOEMI   Es gab
auch andere Ausnahmen wie Vicente Lesser Gutierrez,
der Dinge über unser Haus herausgefunden hat, die nicht
einmal wir wussten. Es war wirklich toll, ihn hier zu haben:
Er ist herumgeschlichen und hat herausgefunden, dass das
Haus anscheinend mal einen Schornstein hatte. Daraufhin
hat er eine Soundinstallation in diesen alten Schornstein auf dem Dach gebaut, so dass wir die Vibrationen der
Reggaeton-Musik im ganzen Haus bis in den Keller hören
konnten. Wir freuen uns sehr über diese Art von Projekten,
aber nicht alle Künstler*innen arbeiten so.

structure on the roof, so we could hear the vibrations of reggaeton music throughout the house, all the way down to the basement. We get very excited about these kinds of projects, but not every artist can do this.

MARLENE   Of course, there's a repetition of space when you realize an exhibition. Even though the given spaces are somehow repetitive, the interactions with or within the rooms can be a big surprise. It might be a gift that keeps on giving inside of your home, the fact that you are able to learn more about your own spaces and see the same rooms in a different light.

INES   In general, spaces have transformative potential. Even in a house like this with four similar floor plans on top of each other, each floor feels different because of different lighting or furniture.   NOEMI   But before a new show, we always invite artists to walk through the space with us, because pictures can only show part of it.   VICTORIA   We invite them to get a feel for the space.   NOEMI   We always tell them, "Hey, everything you see can be discussed together. If you like a

MARLENE   Natürlich gibt es räumliche Wiederholungen, wenn man eine Ausstellung realisiert. Aber auch wenn die gegebenen Räume in gewisser Weise repetitiv sind, kann es völlig überraschende Interaktionen mit oder in den Räumen geben. Mehr über die eigenen Räume zu erfahren und die gleichen Räume in einem anderen Licht zu sehen, kann ein sich immer wieder erneuerndes Geschenk für das Haus sein.

INES   Räume haben generell ein transformatives Potenzial. Selbst in einem Haus wie diesem mit vier ähnlichen Grundrissen übereinander fühlt sich jedes Stockwerk anders an, weil es anders beleuchtet oder anders eingerichtet ist.   NOEMI   Vor jeder neuen Ausstellung laden wir die Künstler*innen ein, die Räumlichkeiten gemeinsam mit uns zu begehen, denn Fotos vermitteln immer nur einen Teil der Realität.   VICTORIA   Wir laden sie ein, sich mit dem Raum vertraut zu machen.   NOEMI   Wir sagen ihnen immer: „Hey, alles, was ihr seht, kann bespielt werden, wenn wir gemeinsam darüber sprechen. Wenn euch ein bestimmter Teil des Hauses oder ein bestimmter Raum gefällt, sagt es uns, und wir werden sehen, was wir tun können." Wir sind immer bereit, das Haus für eine Ausstellung umzugestalten, auch wenn das bedeutet, dass wir unsere Gewohnheiten für eine Weile ändern müssen. Es gab noch keine Ausstellung, für die wir nicht etwas umstellen

particular space, a particular room, tell us and we will see what we can do." We're always willing to adapt the house for a show, even if it means changing our habits for a while. There hasn't been a single show where we haven't had to move things around. But that's part of living here. You have to be open to it. For example, we once removed our dining table for an artist's installation. But if it's needed for a show, we'll do it.

MARLENE   Isn't it funny that in exhibitions we are always looking for transformation from one show to the next, while in everyday life, we often stick to routine and repetition? Even our furniture can be too heavy to move once it has found its place. How do you reconcile the need for continuity in your personal space with the ever-changing nature of exhibitions?

NICOLÁS   Our bedrooms are private, but we're open to changes in shared areas.   NOEMI   For me personally, having a studio space helps maintain balance. We're often out during the day, so coming together in the evening to share a meal and discuss projects is something I look forward to.

131

mussten. Aber das gehört dazu, wenn man hier lebt. Man muss dafür offen sein. Einmal haben wir zum Beispiel für die Installation eines Künstlers unseren Esstisch weggeräumt. Aber wenn es für eine Ausstellung notwendig ist, dann machen wir das.

MARLENE   Es ist irgendwie komisch, dass wir bei Ausstellungen von Mal zu Mal die Veränderung suchen, während unser Alltag oft von Routine und Wiederholung geprägt ist. Unsere Möbel zum Beispiel sind oft zu schwer, um sie zu verrücken, sobald sie ihren Platz gefunden haben. Wie kann es eurer Meinung nach gelingen, das Bedürfnis nach Kontinuität im persönlichen Umfeld mit dem sich ständig wandelnden Charakter von Ausstellungen in Einklang zu bringen?

NICOLÁS   Unsere Zimmer sind privat, aber wir sind offen für Veränderungen in den Gemeinschaftsräumen. NOEMI   Mir persönlich hilft es, ein Atelier zu haben, als Ausgleich. Wir sind tagsüber viel unterwegs, deshalb freue ich mich, wenn wir abends zusammen essen und über unsere Projekte sprechen können.   VERA   Kontinuität hängt davon ab, wie wir unser Wohnen und Zusammenleben organisieren. Wir sind so sehr an das Modell des Privateigentums gewöhnt, wo alle ihren eigenen Raum haben – wir kümmern uns darum, wir organisieren ihn, wir machen

VERA Continuity depends on how we structure our living arrangements and our idea of living together. We're so used to a private property model where everyone has their own space—they take care of it, they organize it, they do what they want with it. This is maybe a more general sense of how things "should" be, and how we are taught that they are. But Palazzina challenges this by creating a collective living and working environment. Continuity doesn't feel so necessary anymore. I've already lived in two different spaces here, and I feel completely at home. It's a way of testing what it means to share a space and to rethink the concept of private property. Stability can also come from a social structure.   **VICTORIA** I totally agree, because I think it highlights the importance of trust and intuition.

MARLENE Trust and intuition are subjective, but they're also crucial in a collective setting. We've already touched on the idea of trust as a way of working, knowing that other people are there to work *with* you. Is there such a thing as collective intuition in order to make decisions together, like choosing artists or dividing tasks? How do trust and democracy interact in your collaborative efforts?

132

damit, was wir wollen. So oder so ähnlich stellen wir uns vor, wie die Dinge sein sollten, und so wird es uns beigebracht. Aber Palazzina stellt das in Frage, indem wir ein kollektives Wohn- und Arbeitsumfeld schaffen. Kontinuität ist dann nicht mehr so entscheidend. Ich habe hier schon in zwei verschiedenen Räumen gewohnt und fühle mich überall zu Hause. Auf diese Weise können wir damit experimentieren, was es bedeutet, einen Raum zu teilen und das Konzept des Privateigentums zu überdenken. Stabilität kann auch durch ein soziales Gefüge entstehen.   **VICTORIA** Ich stimme dir voll und ganz zu, weil deutlich wird, wie wichtig Vertrauen und Intuition sind.

MARLENE Vertrauen und Intuition sind subjektiv, aber in einem kollektiven Umfeld von entscheidender Bedeutung. Wir haben bereits über die Idee des Vertrauens als Grundlage für die Zusammenarbeit gesprochen – das Wissen, dass andere Menschen da sind, um *mit* einem zusammenzuarbeiten. Gibt es so etwas wie eine kollektive Intuition, um gemeinsam Entscheidungen zu treffen, wie beispielsweise die Auswahl von Künstler*innen oder die Aufgabenteilung? Wie interagieren Vertrauen und demokratische Prinzipien in euren Gemeinschaftsprojekten?

VICTORIA   It's a mix of both. It's like a hive mind—the more people involved, the more ideas and artists come into play. Trust builds because everyone contributes and feels responsible for what they're good at, for example knowing a lot about sound, how to build an exhibition, or writing texts. I think that trust is also something that has been built in a way.
NOEMI   Trust grows with care.

MARLENE   A lot of terms you use to describe the collective are quite functional and resemble that of a domestic setting—care, living, sharing spaces. Even though not everyone lives here, it really feels like a *living* organism.

NOEMI   Each person brings their personal experience and knowledge, which allows us to work with a lot of people from all over Switzerland and from different backgrounds, or to come up with new ideas for putting specific artists together. One person alone would never be able to come up with that. Through these kinds of discussions and by sharing insights we can choose our own program. There are no grand curatorial concepts; intuition plays a big role in this sense.

133

VICTORIA   Es ist eine Mischung aus beidem. Es ist wie eine Art Schwarmintelligenz – je mehr Leute mitmachen, desto mehr Ideen und Künstler*innen kommen ins Spiel. Vertrauen entsteht, weil alle etwas beitragen und sich für das verantwortlich fühlen, worin sie gut sind – zum Beispiel viel über Tontechnik wissen, wissen, wie man eine Ausstellung aufbaut oder Texte schreibt. Ich denke, dass das Vertrauen auch etwas ist, das sich aufbaut.   NOEMI   Vertrauen wächst durch Fürsorge.

MARLENE   Viele Begriffe, die ihr benutzt, um das Kollektiv zu beschreiben, sind sehr funktional und ähneln denen einer häuslichen Umgebung – Fürsorge, Zusammenleben, gemeinschaftliche Raumnutzung. Auch wenn nicht alle hier leben, fühlt es sich wirklich wie ein *lebendiger* Organismus an.

NOEMI   Dass jede Person ihre persönlichen Erfahrungen und ihr Wissen einbringt, ermöglicht es uns, mit vielen Menschen aus der ganzen Schweiz und mit unterschiedlichen Backgrounds zusammenzuarbeiten oder Künstler*innen in überraschenden Konstellationen auszustellen. Eine Person alleine wäre dazu nie in der Lage. Indem wir diskutieren und Wissen austauschen, können wir unser eigenes Programm entwickeln. Es gibt keine grossen kuratorischen Konzepte, stattdessen spielt Intuition eine massgebliche Rolle.

MARLENE   This seems to bring out a personal aspect, as
your artistic and/or curatorial practices extend beyond
the house into your own work. You bring these different
kinds of collective spaces back into your personal space.
Do you find that being part of this collective has influ-
enced your personal work?

VICTORIA   When I'm invited to another offspace, I go with
a deep sense of gratitude because I know how hard it is to
create something like this.

MARLENE   That's so nice, because it influences how you
enter another space, how you interact and work with others, and how you exhibit your work.

INES   Being here, where everything is interconnected—
living, working, discussing—has made me more aware that
creativity doesn't happen on demand. We've created a more
open environment where ideas can develop naturally, rather
than being forced. This is something that I've also taken into
my own practice.

134

MARLENE   Das scheint einen persönlichen Aspekt
zu betonen, denn eure künstlerischen und/oder kuratorischen Praktiken gehen über die Grenzen des Hauses
hinaus und setzen sich in eurer eigenen Arbeit fort.
Ihr transferiert diese verschiedenen Arten von kollektiven Räumen in euren persönlichen Raum. Glaubt
ihr, dass die Zugehörigkeit zu diesem Kollektiv eure
individuelle Arbeit geprägt hat?

VICTORIA   Wenn ich in einen anderen Offspace eingeladen
werde, gehe ich mit einem tiefen Gefühl der Dankbarkeit
hin, weil ich weiss, wie schwer es ist, so etwas zu verwirk-
lichen.

MARLENE   Das ist ein sehr schöner Gedanke, denn er
hat Einfluss darauf, wie man sich einen Raum erschliesst,
wie man mit anderen interagiert und zusammenarbei-
tet und wie man seine Arbeit präsentiert.

INES   Hier zu sein, wo alles miteinander verwoben ist –
leben, arbeiten, diskutieren – hat mir noch mehr bewusst
gemacht, dass Kreativität nicht auf Abruf entsteht. Wir
haben ein offeneres Umfeld geschaffen, in dem sich Ideen
auf natürliche Weise entwickeln können und nicht
forciert werden. Das habe ich viel in meine eigene Praxis
übernommen.

MARLENE   Work doesn't stop when you leave the studio or the museum—it usually never does. So, when you're together after a day in the studio or elsewhere, you can still think collectively and productively about your individual work. Does this blur the lines between personal and collective practice?

VICTORIA   That's a question of setting boundaries, which is crucial. Sometimes you need to say, "I can't do this right now. I have too much on my plate." Since there are so many of us, others can step in when needed.   NOEMI   Turning off your phone helps, too!   KELLY   We don't all organize every show. For each exhibition, some members are more involved than others. Responsibilities are divided so that we can take breaks when needed. We help each other out, which keeps things manageable. We are all in a similar situation with our practices or our jobs. So it's actually quite smooth.

MARLENE   What are some of the practical challenges of sustaining your collective space that are usually less smooth?

135

MARLENE   Die Arbeit hört nicht auf, wenn ihr das Atelier oder das Museum verlasst – sie hört normalerweise nie auf. Wenn ihr also nach einem Tag im Atelier oder anderswo zusammen seid, könnt ihr immer noch gemeinsam und produktiv über eure individuelle Arbeit nachdenken. Verwischt das die Grenzen zwischen persönlicher und kollektiver Praxis?

VICTORIA   Das ist eine Frage der Abgrenzung, und der müssen wir uns stellen. Manchmal müssen wir sagen: „Ich kann das gerade nicht übernehmen. Ich habe zu viel um die Ohren." Da wir so viele sind, können andere einspringen, falls nötig.   NOEMI   Das Handy auszuschalten hilft auch!   KELLY   Wir sind nicht alle an jeder Ausstellung beteiligt. Bei jedem Projekt sind einige Mitglieder stärker involviert als andere. Die Zuständigkeiten sind so verteilt, dass wir, wenn nötig, Pausen einlegen können. Wir helfen uns gegenseitig, so dass alles machbar bleibt. Wir sind alle in einer ähnlichen Situation, was unsere Praxis oder unsere Jobs betrifft. Es läuft also eigentlich ziemlich reibungslos.

MARLENE   Was sind einige der praktischen Herausforderungen in Bezug auf euren Gemeinschaftsraum? Was läuft normalerweise nicht reibungslos?

NICOLÁS   The rent situation is crazy. There are a lot of unused spaces, but there's no political interest in making them available.   NOEMI   The rigid divide between living and working spaces is still a problem. Cultural funding often doesn't cover operational costs, but in our case, our living situation is intertwined with running the space.   NICOLÁS   We're often faced with the need to plan programs far in advance, sometimes a year in advance, which can be counterintuitive to the way we naturally work. In some ways, it's like we're rolling a ball, trying to keep the momentum going while dealing with different schedules and expectations. This pressure isn't just about meeting deadlines; it's also about the day-to-day challenges of maintaining our space—paying rent, managing resources. These demands can create a tension between our idealistic vision of how we want to work and the reality of what needs to be done. It can be easy to lose that sense of spontaneity. Sometimes, you have to step back and imagine what others in the collective might be feeling or wanting to do, especially when we're not all together in the same room or on the same page. This situation is layered with the different experiences and stages we're each going through. Some

NICOLÁS   Der Immobilienmarkt ist völlig verrückt. Es gibt viele ungenutzte Flächen, aber es gibt kein politisches Interesse, diese nutzbar zu machen.   NOEMI   Die strikte Trennung zwischen Wohnen und Arbeiten ist immer noch ein Problem. Die Kulturförderung deckt oft nicht die Betriebskosten, aber in unserem Fall ist unsere Wohnsituation mit dem Betrieb des Raumes verflochten.   NICOLÁS   Wir sind oft mit der Notwendigkeit konfrontiert, Programme weit im Voraus zu planen, manchmal ein Jahr im Voraus, was unserer natürlichen Arbeitsweise zuwiderlaufen kann. Es ist, als würden wir einen Ball ins Rollen bringen und versuchen, ihn in Schwung zu halten, während wir mit verschiedenen Zeitplänen und Erwartungen konfrontiert sind. Dabei geht es nicht nur um das Einhalten von Fristen, sondern auch um die täglichen Herausforderungen im Hinblick auf den Unterhalt unserer Räumlichkeiten – Miete zahlen, Ressourcen verwalten. Dieser Druck kann zu Spannungen führen zwischen unserer idealistischen Vorstellung, wie wir arbeiten wollen, und der Realität dessen, was getan werden muss. Es kann leicht passieren, dass die Spontaneität verloren geht. Manchmal müssen wir einen Schritt zurücktreten und uns vorstellen, wie sich die anderen in der Gruppe fühlen oder was sie tun wollen, vor allem, wenn wir nicht alle zusammensitzen oder gleicher Meinung sind. Diese Situation wird durch die unterschiedlichen Erfahrungen und Lebensphasen, die wir alle durchlaufen,

years are better than others for each of us, and this fluctu-
ation adds another layer of complexity to how we operate.
Sometimes it's almost like running a company, where we're
constantly adapting to each other's needs and situations.
NOEMI   I agree, but every time we've faced challenges, like
having to move, we always asked ourselves if we wanted to
stay together, if we still wanted to date or be life partners.
Each time we realized that what we have is really nice. We
decided to stay together because we believe in something.
VICTORIA   Communication has a lot to do with it. We make
sure to speak up if we need help or can't take something on.
That's why we always have a backup person now, so if someone is going to look after an artist for a project, we always
make sure there's someone there as a backup.

> MARLENE   It sounds like you're describing life itself,
> where trust and collaboration help to navigate systemic
> pressures like rent and funding. It's somehow very realis-
> tic and pragmatic, but at the same time, I wonder if I would
> call it counterintuitive?

137

noch komplizierter. Für uns alle sind manche Jahre besser
als andere, und diese Schwankungen sorgen dafür,
dass unsere Arbeitsweise noch komplexer wird. Manchmal
ist es fast so, als würde man ein Unternehmen leiten, in
dem man sich ständig an die Bedürfnisse und Situationen
der anderen anpassen muss.   NOEMI   Ich stimme dir
zu, aber jedes Mal, wenn wir vor Herausforderungen standen,
wie etwa einem Umzug, haben wir uns gefragt, ob wir
zusammenbleiben wollen, ob wir noch eine Beziehung
führen oder Lebenspartner*innen sein wollen. Jedes
Mal wurde uns bewusst, dass das, was wir haben, wirklich
schön ist. Wir haben uns entschieden, zusammenzu-
bleiben, weil wir an etwas glauben.   VICTORIA   Kommunikation spielt eine grosse Rolle. Wir sprechen offen an,
wenn wir Hilfe benötigen oder etwas nicht übernehmen
können. Deshalb haben wir jetzt immer eine Person als
Unterstützung. Wenn sich also jemand um eine*n Künstler*in für ein Projekt kümmert, stellen wir sicher, dass immer
jemand als Backup da ist.

> MARLENE   Es klingt, als würdet ihr das Leben selbst
> beschreiben, wo Vertrauen und Zusammenarbeit
> helfen, Systemzwänge wie Miete und Finanzierung zu
> bewältigen. Das klingt irgendwie sehr realistisch
> und pragmatisch, aber gleichzeitig frage ich mich, ob
> es nicht kontraintuitiv ist?

NICOLÁS   The systemic forces are not really intuitive. Well, maybe they are, but they follow another kind of intuition.

MARLENE   The challenge is to make the system work for you, rather than just working within it. With so many minds working together, it seems that you might have more opportunities to activate things that might otherwise be impossible individually?

VICTORIA   We've learned that the trust within our group doesn't always extend to external systems and people. We've realized that the structure that we've built for ourselves works really well. It's a reminder of the trust we have in our collective, and sometimes that means saying no to other projects or deciding to do things in a different way.

MARLENE   So the collective mind doesn't always translate to other spaces?

VICTORIA   No, that's why it's important to recognize our strengths and use our collective freedom to say no when

138

NICOLÁS   Die Kräfte, die im System wirken, sind nicht wirklich intuitiv. Vielleicht sind sie es, aber sie folgen einer anderen Art von Intuition.

MARLENE   Die Herausforderung besteht darin, das System für sich arbeiten zu lassen, anstatt nur innerhalb des Systems zu arbeiten. Wenn so viele Köpfe zusammenarbeiten, hat man dann die Möglichkeit, bestimmte Vorhaben zu realisieren, die für die*en Einzelne*n vielleicht unmöglich wären?

VICTORIA   Wir haben gelernt, dass das Vertrauen, das wir innerhalb unserer Gruppe geniessen, sich nicht immer auf externe Systeme und Personen erstreckt. Wir haben festgestellt, dass die Struktur, die wir uns aufgebaut haben, wirklich gut funktioniert. Sie erinnert uns an das Vertrauen, das wir in unser Kollektiv haben, und manchmal bedeutet das, nein zu anderen Projekten zu sagen oder zu entscheiden, Dinge auf unsere eigene Art und Weise zu tun.

MARLENE   Das kollektive Bewusstsein ist also nicht immer auf andere Räume übertragbar?

VICTORIA   Nein, deshalb ist es wichtig, dass wir unsere Stärken erkennen und unsere kollektive Freiheit nutzen, um nein zu sagen, wenn es nötig ist. Schliesslich arbeiten

necessary. After all, the work we do is voluntary and unpaid.
NOEMI   That's also the advantage of being an offspace compared to a bigger institution. We can move more freely and if
we don't want to collaborate with someone, we can just do
whatever we feel like doing. We can follow our ideas without
being tied to institutional expectations.   INES   As we grow
and become more professional, an institutional way of working is not too far away. But it's important to keep that freedom
and not get caught up in too many restrictions and the rules
that usually come with a more professional environment.

MARLENE   What are your hopes or visions for Palazzina
in the coming years, now that you've reached this five-
year milestone?

SIMONE   To win the lottery and buy a house.

139

wir alle ehrenamtlich und unentgeltlich.   NOEMI   Das
ist auch der Vorteil eines Offspaces gegenüber einer
grösseren Institution. Wir können freier agieren, und wenn
wir mit jemandem nicht zusammenarbeiten wollen, können
wir einfach das machen, wonach uns der Sinn steht.
Wir können unseren Ideen folgen, ohne an institutionelle
Vorgaben gebunden zu sein.   INES   Je mehr wir wachsen
und je professioneller wir arbeiten, desto mehr nähern
wir uns einer institutionellen Arbeitsweise an. Es ist jedoch
wichtig, sich eine gewisse Freiheit zu bewahren und sich
nicht zu vielen Einschränkungen und Regeln zu unterwerfen,
die gewöhnlich mit einem professionelleren Umfeld
einhergehen.

MARLENE   Welche Hoffnungen oder Visionen habt
ihr für das Palazzina in den nächsten Jahren, jetzt wo ihr
diesen Meilenstein von fünf Jahren erreicht habt?

SIMONE   Im Lotto gewinnen und ein Haus kaufen.

1   As a modular format that transcends the fixed structure of a house,
     On Foot came to life in 2023, developed and designed by Ester
     Alemayehu Hatle, Emil Hvelplund Kristiansen, and Jakub Andrzejewski.
     Conceived as an extension to the exhibition space, the structure is a
     mobile and interchangeable stacking system made from hempcrete
     blocks and scaffolding. As a flexible pavilion, it can be adapted to a
     variety of exhibition contexts without the need for a fixed location. The
     aim of this approach is to continually rethink exhibition displays and
     formats and to enter into dialogue with a diverse audience.

2   As part of a performance, San Keller was given Palazzina's house key
     for the duration of the exhibition *Palazzina #9* (2021). The work, titled
     Alemannengasse, included the house key and a flashlight. The artist
     wanted to temporarily hand over both objects to neighbors in order
     for them to have access to the show and to the living spaces of the
     Palazzina residents. Although Keller's work was only visible through
     the description of the work, he created space for the unknown and
     sparked a discourse about trust and imagination.

140

1   Als modulares Format, das über die feste Struktur eines Hauses
     hinausgeht, wurde *On Foot* 2023 von Ester Alemayehu Hatle, Emil
     Hvelplund Kristiansen und Jakub Andrzejewski entwickelt. Die
     Struktur, die aus einem mobilen und austauschbaren Stapelsystem
     aus Hanfbetonblöcken und Gerüsten besteht, wurde als Erwei-
     terung des Ausstellungsraums konzipiert. Als flexibler Pavillon kann
     sie an eine Vielzahl von Ausstellungskontexten angepasst werden,
     ohne an einen festen Standort gebunden zu sein. Ziel dieses Ansatzes
     ist es, Ausstellungsdisplays und -formate immer wieder neu zu
     überdenken und mit einem vielfältigen Publikum in Dialog zu treten.

2   Im Rahmen einer Performance erhielt San Keller für die Dauer der
     Ausstellung *Palazzina #9* (2021) den Hausschlüssel des Palazzina.
     Die Arbeit *Alemannengasse* bestand aus dem Hausschlüssel
     und einer Taschenlampe. Beide Objekte wollte der Künstler vorüber-
     gehend den Nachbar*innen aushändigen, damit diese Zugang zur
     Ausstellung und zu den Wohnräumen der Palazzina-Bewohner*innen
     hatten. Obwohl Kellers Arbeit nur durch die Beschreibung erfahr-
     bar war, schuf er Raum für das Unbekannte und regte einen Diskurs
     über Vertrauen und die Vorstellungskraft an.

As a curator and art historian, MARLENE MARTI BÜRGI works between Bern, Basel, and Lausanne. In 2016, she completed a master's degree in museology and collection history at Leiden University in the Netherlands. She works on different exhibition projects, runs the offspace *Bad Posture* in Lausanne, and regularly writes texts on contemporary exhibitions and artists.

141

MARLENE MARTI BÜRGI arbeitet als Kuratorin und Kunsthistorikerin zwischen Bern, Basel und Lausanne. 2016 erlangte sie einen Master-abschluss in Museologie und Sammlungsgeschichte an der Universität Leiden in den Niederlanden. Sie betreut verschiedene Ausstellungs-projekte, leitet den Offspace *Bad Posture* in Lausanne und verfasst regelmässig Texte zu aktuellen Ausstellungen und Künstler*innen.

Appendix

Exhibitions

Palazzina #1   30.10–30.11.2019
          Sofía Durrieu
          Rebecca Kunz

Palazzina #2   13.12.2019–12.1.2020
          Marilou Bal
          Sara Gassmann
          Séverine Heizmann (Performance)

Palazzina #3   13.2–1.3.2020
          Melanie Akeret
          Haydée Marin
          Hannes Zulauf

Palazzina #4   *Surgeons and Gluttons*
          12–29.3.2020
          Caterina De Nicola
          Philip Ortelli
          Mitchell Anderson (Text)

Palazzina #5   8–26.4.2020
          Katrin Niedermeier
          & Co.

Palazzina #6   *Neither the either nor the or are*
          places to be
          6–24.5.2020
          Brigham Baker
          Nina Rieben

Palazzina #7   *Drawing Sessions.*
          Basel Berlin Bude
          3–21.6.2020
          Zara Idelson
          Claudia & Julia Müller

Schweizergasse 2, Basel ⇒ Alemannengasse 60, Basel

Palazzina #8   17.9–11.10.2020
          Caroline Bachmann
          Chloé Delarue
          Natacha Donzé
          Camille Lacroix
          Kaspar Ludwig
          Dominic Michel
          Emanuel Rossetti
          Grégory Sugnaux

Palazzina #9   20.2–25.4.2021
          Camille Dumond
          Leolie Greet
          San Keller
          Philémon Otth
          Sara Ravelli

Palazzina #10	22.5–15.8.2021 Vesna Bilanović Amélie Bodenmann Valentin Carron Elise Corpataux Mariana Murcia
Palazzina #11	*From Submersion to Subversion* 19.9–17.10.2021 Giada Olivotto (Guest Curator) Camilla Paolino (Guest Curator) Lula Broglio Maïté Chénière Giorgia Garzilli Maya Hottarek Viola Leddi
Palazzina #12	4.12.2021–30.1.2022 Andreas Dobler Judith Kakon Val Minnig Ivan Mitrović Julie Monot Dario Zeo (Text)
Palazzina #13	13.2–13.3.2022 Djellza Azemi Tiphanie Kim Mall Nusser Glazova Remy Ugarte Vallejos
Palazzina #14	1.4–1.5.2022 Marisabel Arias Camille Farrah Buhler Anne-Laure Franchette Gilles Jacot Francesca Mangold
Palazzina Backyard	21.4–19.6.2022 Sophie Yerly
Palazzina #15	*Bye-Bye Alemannengasse* 3–19.6.2022 Leonardo Bürgi Tenorio Pauline Coquart Bastien Gachet Lucas Herzig Daniel Kurth Lena Laguna Mirjam Plattner

Alemannengasse 60, Basel ⇒ Baslerstrasse 321, Allschwil

Palazzina #16	*Hello Baslerstrasse!* 1–18.9.2022 Livio Casanova LapTopRadio (Performance) Lorraine Baylac (Dinner)
Palazzina #17	*The Fridge Show* 10.12.2022–29.1.2023 Anaïs Nariman Aïk Charles Benjamin Lysann König Léa Katharina Meier Anastasia Pavlou Alan Schmalz Linus Weber
Palazzina #18	*Parallelmontage* 3–19.3.2023 Phoenix Atala Lara and Noa Castro TJ Cuthand Tobias Dirty Núria Güell Mónica Heller Valentina Parati Roman Selim Khereddine Leevi Toija
Palazzina #19	*The Day Before* 14.4–7.5.2023 Alex Ghandour Eli Maria Lundgaard Marta Margnetti Mathilde Rosier Paulo Wirz
Palazzina #20	*Counter Loopholes* 26.5–8.7.2023 Vicente Lesser Gutierrez Ingo Niermann Paula Santomé
Palazzina #21	*Exploded* 26.8–16.10.2023 Adrien Chevalley Laim Kim Tim Kummer Ronja Svaneborg Baker Wardlaw
Screening Program at CAN, Centre d'art Neuchâtel	*Lost, Found, Cut and Stolen* 13.1.2024 Josefin Arnell Mia Sanchez Carolina Sandvik Thales Pessoa Sara Magenheimer

Palazzina #22	*I Am Blue!* 20.1–25.2.2024 Simon Fahrni Ray Hegelbach Sina Oberhänsli Hanna Rochereau Ana Bălan (Performance)
Palazzina #23	*Echochambers* 6.4–12.5.2024 Andreas Kalbermatter Dominic Michel (Text)
Palazzina #24	*Scarecrows Don't Talk* 31.5–7.7.2024 Salome Jokhadze Jennifer Merlyn Scherler Rhona Mühlebach
Palazzina #25	*Gravity's End* 9–16.6.2024 Gina Proenza
Palazzina #26	*Soft Collisions* 21.9.2024 Anina Müller Ernestyna Orlowska Juliette Uzor Victor Delétraz X Schneeberger
Palazzina #27	*Found Anatomy* 8.11–15.12.2024 Lithic Alliance Tomás Maglione Guadalupe Ruiz

Locations

Schweizergasse 2
4054 Basel

1.7.2019–30.6.2020

Apartment building next to the Zoo

4 Floors
4 Apartments
4 Kitchens
5 Bathrooms
1 Basement

Members / Tenants

○ Géraldine Honauer
○ Ines Tondar
○ Kelly Tissot
○ Luca Rossi Dossi
○ Mathieu Dafflon
○ Noemi Pfister
○ Simone Holliger
○ Tilda
○ Victoria Holdt

Exhibitions

Palazzina #1–7

Alemannengasse 60
4058 Basel

1.7.2020–31.6.2022
Residential building next to the Rhine

4 Floors
1 Kitchen
4 Bathrooms
2 Basements

Members / Tenants

○ Ester Alemayehu Hatle
○ Géraldine Honauer
○ Ines Tondar
○ Joaquim Cantor Miranda
○ Joan Pallé
○ Katrin Niedermeier
○ Kelly Tissot
○ Luca Rossi Dossi
○ Mathieu Dafflon
○ Nicolás Sarmiento
○ Noemi Pfister
○ Simone Holliger
○ Tilda
○ Victoria Holdt

Exhibitions

Palazzina #8–15

Baslerstrasse 321
4123 Allschwil

since 1.7.2022

Apartment building next to
Lindenplatz

4 Floors
4 Apartments
3 Kitchens
7 Bathrooms
1 Attic
1 Basement
1 Garden House

Members / Tenants

○ Á. Birna Björnsdóttir
○ Ester Alemayehu Hatle
○ Ines Tondar
○ Ivan Mitrović
○ Jakub Andrzejewski
○ Katrin Niedermeier
○ Madeleine Noraas
○ Mathieu Dafflon
○ Noemi Pfister
○ Nicolás Sarmiento
○ Simone Holliger
○ Tilda
○ Vera Mühlebach
○ Victoria Holdt

Exhibitions

Palazzina #16–27
ongoing

On Foot
Various Locations

26.5–10.6.2023 (Palazzina, Baslerstrasse 321, Allschwil)

12.6–17.6.2023 (Basel Social Club, Former Mayonnaise Factory, Franck Areal Basel)

26.8–16.10.2023 (Lindenplatz, Allschwil)

9.–16.6.2024 (Basel Social Club, Farmland, Bruderholz, Basel-Landschaft)

21.9.2024 (Former Post Office, Baslerstrasse 103, Allschwil)

Mobile structure

380 Full Bricks
36 Half Bricks
96 Meter Scaffolding Pipes
60 Scaffolding Joints
25 Scaffolding Feet
2 Doors

Developed & designed by

○ Ester Alemayehu Hatle
○ Emil Hvelplund Kristiansen
○ Jakub Andrzejewski

Exhibitions

Palazzina #20
Palazzina #21
Palazzina #25
Palazzina #26

Exhibition Views
Selection 2019–25

List of Works

| 17 | | ☐ Baker Wardlaw, *Post*, 2023
Flags and hardware |

| 18 | 19 | ☐ Francesca Mangold, *Reunion of antennae*, 2019–22
Cotton and acrylic fabrics, stuffing, name badges, digital prints on paper, dry leaves, wood and soil |

| 20 | 21 | ☐ Valentin Carron, *Consolatio*, 2021
Photopolymer resin |

| 22 | 23 | ☐ Anne-Laure Franchette, *Au service de la beauté*, 2022
T-Shirt
☐ Judith Kakon, *After Commons*, 2021
Steel, garlic, multi-part |

| 24 | 25 | ☐ Anina Müller, *I Have Nothing to Wear*, 2024
Performance
☐ Jennifer Merlyn Scherler, *Lipsync is not enough (Forest Fae)*, 2023
Styrodur, acrystal, digital print on archival matte paper |

| 26 | 27 | ☐ Tim Kummer, *Three day holiday*, 2023, chewing gum Jesus, chewing gum packages
☐ Laim Kim, *Embaumer*, 2023
Aluminium and steel
☐ Paula Santomé, *Ecdysis (I–XI)*, 2023
Aluminium |

| 28 | 29 | ☐ Maya Hottarek, *Today I Offer You Everything*, 2021
Ceramics, incense, rope |

| 30 | 31 | ☐ Ana Bălan, 2024
Performance
☐ Marisabel Arias, *I wish, I would like girls not be afraid of liking girls*, 2022
LED fan, plugs and electricity |

| 32 | 33 | ☐ Caroline Bachmann, *Serie portrait artistes*, 2015–20
Oil on canvas
☐ Juliette Uzor, *Duet (hi how are you)*, 2024
Performance |

34 35   □ *On Foot* at Basel Social Club, 2024
    □ Gina Proenza, *Gravity's End*, 2024
    □ Philémon Otth, *Breakout*, 2021
    Steel, painting and plaster
    □ Lucas Herzig, *Untitled*, 2021
    Papier-mâché

36 37   □ Lucas Herzig, *E spesso intendo sempre*, 2022
    Found objects
    □ X Schneeberger, 2024
    Performance

38 39   □ Andreas Kalbermatter, *Pumpkin*, 2024
    Helmet, stretched fabric on cardboard and inkjet print on artist's pedestal
    □ Andreas Kalbermatter, *Target color suck*, 2024
    Acrylic on canvas
    □ Andreas Kalbermatter, *Arrangement with eye and horse*, 2024
    Inkjet transfer and acrylic on canvas
    □ Bastien Gachet, *To Cringe*, 2019
    Video, color, sound, 3:28 min

40 41   □ Gilles Jacot, *Schulterklopfer Einheit / Backslapper Unit*, 2022
    Wire coat hangers
    □ Julie Monot, *Lovers*, 2021
    Glazed stoneware

42 43   □ Anaïs Nariman Aïk, *J'espère te revoir bientôt*, 2022
    Pencil and ballpoint on paper, fired glazed clay and magnets

44 45   □ Andreas Dobler, *Chthonox*, 2009
    Acrylic, spray paint, oil on canvas

46 47   □ Leolie Greet, *Seeking Traces, I Left Mine*, 2021
    Silicon, pigment, plaster, cotton, polystyrol, polystyrol-glass, steel, collected plants and crystal necklace
    □ Dominic Michel, *Untitled*, 2020
    UV-printed flag

48 49   □ Sara Ravelli, *Tamed Love*, 2020
    Quilted fabrics, nylon, unfired clay, satin, polyester, rope, salt, iron structure and hair pins
    □ Haydée Marin, *H&M*, 2019

| 50 51 | ☐ | Guadalupe Ruiz, *Hermano*, 2024
DV, 23:10 min. |

52 53	☐	*On Foot* at Lindenplatz, 2023
	☐	Tim Kummer, *Wallhug*, 2023 Ceramic wall anchors, metal rods and nuts
	☐	Philip Ortelli, *Not being straight*, 2019 Aluminium ladder and hinges

54 55	☐	Caterina De Nicola & Philip Ortelli, *Jesus Christ is junior cunt*, 2020 Hay, acrylic paint, squid ink spaghetti, latex and cowboy hat
	☐	Caterina De Nicola, *Untitled*, 2020 Denim patchwork, wooden frame, hay, acrylic paint and squid ink spaghetti
	☐	Natacha Donzé, *Emotional forecast*, 2020 Acrylic on canvas

| 56 57 | ☐ | Paulo Wirz, *Fonte*, 2023
Bronze casts, nails, red thread and
beads |
| | ☐ | Rhona Mühlebach, *Ditch Me –
Character Scroll*, 2023
Digital print on linen, wood |

| 58 59 | ☐ | Mónica Heller, *El gato sangrante y
el corazón barbudo*, 2019
2D animation video, color, sound,
6:03 min |

| 60 61 | ☐ | Anastasia Pavlou, *Anastasia, Leah,
Mathilde*, 2021
Oil and gesso on canvas |
| | ☐ | Djellza Azemi, *Home Is Where the
Ghost Is*, 2022
Brick and wood |

| 62 63 | ☐ | Val Minnig, *Clicc Clicc*, 2021
Ceramics on wood |
| | ☐ | Amélie Bodenmann, *Rose*, 2021
Tin |

| 64 | ☐ | Remy Ugarte Vallejos, *Guides,
guards and grounds*, 2022
Ceramics, wood, vinyl and chains |

Imprint

Palazzina. Ring Everywhere. Überall klingeln

palazzina

Palazzina, Baslerstrasse 321, 4123 Allschwil, Switzerland
palazzina.ch

Editors	Palazzina: Á. Birna Björnsdóttir Ester Alemayehu Hatle Ines Tondar Ivan Mitrović Jakub Andrzejewski Kelly Tissot Madeleine Noraas Mathieu Dafflon Nicolás Sarmiento Noemi Pfister Simone Holliger Vera Mühlebach Victoria Holdt
Translation & Copy Editing	Good & Cheap Art Translators, Berlin (dt., en.) Fanny Lami, Marseille (fr.) Rosanna McLaughlin, St-Leonards-on-Sea (en.)
Book Design	Martina Brassel, Zürich
Paper	ColorPlan Candy Pink, Profibulk
Typeface	Konstruktiv (Martin Andereggen)
Photographs	Finn Curry (pp. 17, 26, 27, 30, 38, 42, 43, 50, 51, 56, 57, 58, 59, 60) Guadalupe Ruiz (pp. 18, 19, 20, 21, 22, 23, 28, 29, 31, 32, 35, 36, 39, 40, 41, 44, 45, 46, 48, 55, 61, 62, 63, 64) Martina Brassel (p. 1) Thalles Piaget (pp. 24, 33, 37, 160) Palazzina (pp. 34, 47, 49, 52, 53, 54)
Published by	Mousse Publishing Contrappunto s.r.l. Via Pier Candido Decembrio 28, 20137, Milan–Italy
Distributed by	Mousse Publishing moussemagazine.it
First Edition Print Run	2025 750 copies
Printed in Switzerland by	TBS, La Buona Stampa sa 6963 Pregassona
	ISBN 978-88-6749-684-6 25 CHF / 25 Euro / 30 Dollar
	© 2025 Mousse Publishing, Palazzina, the artists, the authors of the texts

Many thanks to the supporters of this publication and to those who wish to remain unnamed.

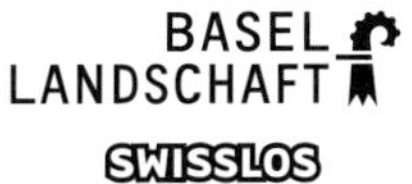 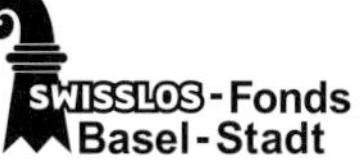

Our gratitude goes to all the artists we have worked with, to everyone who contributed with their ideas and their warmth to the development of our space, to the generous supporters who made this project possible and especially to the precious and caring people who accompanied the realization of this publication.

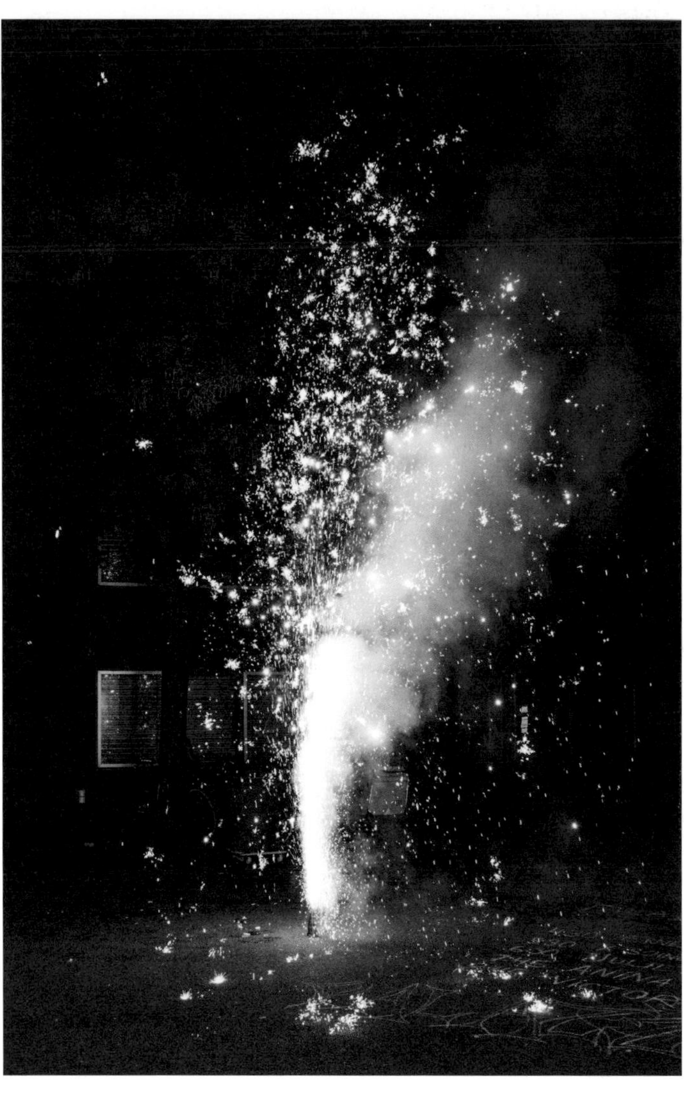